Ce livre appartient à

_____

Apprendre l'anglais en s'amusant avec les mots mêlés !

Ce livre contient **1000 mots** répartis dans 50 grilles, un **lexique** Anglais-Français et les **solutions** en fin d'ouvrage.

Pour donner un sens à votre apprentissage, les mots ont été minutieusement choisis et sont classés par thèmes pour aborder tous les contextes du quotidien.

Comme l'oral est très important dans l'apprentissage d'une langue, ce livre contient un lien (page 54) qui vous permettra d'accéder à un **audio** pour écouter et répéter la prononciation des mots que vous aurez appris.

Comment ça marche ?

1. Notez la traduction des mots que vous connaissez dans l'espace dédié.
2. Pour le nouveau vocabulaire, aidez-vous du lexique page 55.
3. Recherchez les mots en anglais dans les grilles.
4. Écoutez la prononciation à l'aide de l'audio page 54.

Ce jeu de mots mêlés a fait ses preuves pour faciliter la mémorisation du vocabulaire anglais par le jeu.

D1727590

Days & Months

```
K A K J U J O S X I U I M N S O P B W
R T Z J C E O Y A D S E U T B K Y D Q
F P F Q R Y L J Y R A U R B E F A Z F
C C Q E N H A P J Q G Q N G I J D Y S
G S A P R I L D N X J E M G D I S M E
X P L F G Q H O S U R O Y Z L J R D P
U N H C R A M Y F E N H F H B K U N T
Q Q Z J U N E A B D N O A J I Q H E E
D U T B N X C D A T Y D Z O L G T K M
E U C E V O E Y S I B A E F W C F E B
C Q Y M A Y V A D J Y Z D W Q S J E E
E F I M N F T E X G U T T I T E Y W R
M A T J D U E N M G B L S H R X R Z R
B P S Y R F K S M B J D Y U F F A Y N
E B P D B G M C F M E X N J G O U I T
R V A I A X R V Y W Y R G J U U N W W
P Y T U L O C T O B E R T Z B R A C W
A C I F C T C R Y A D N U S U W J W H
C H O N T M I S F S F A J Y F B N S E
```

MONDAY	Lundi	TUESDAY	_____
WEDNESDAY	_____	THURSDAY	_____
FRIDAY	_____	SATURDAY	_____
SUNDAY	_____	JANUARY	_____
FEBRUARY	_____	MARCH	_____
APRIL	_____	MAY	_____
JUNE	_____	JULY	_____
AUGUST	_____	SEPTEMBER	_____
OCTOBER	_____	NOVEMBER	_____
DECEMBER	_____	WEEKEND	_____

Solutions p. 67

Weather

```
N O Y D N G S V E Y H W F I Y E H R O
M Z L I E M Z H Z A T S P R I N G L T
B N A D R Y F J T R M S A R H V M P O
D R C O F K D T H W U I J T N T T L Q
D Z Y D U O L C L M N E A U O M B F T
W E F K A V X C M B C U E D R Z N H F
I S G O Z J Q E O G R L J O U F G T C
N H W O Z Q R W B E H H T V I U V S N
D Y M O C N S V S V L S F L O P H A M
Y O N L N D M D O I L C S R H O T C H
X N T N J S L U W E M L D F R J X R B
F F E X U O V I T D F C J Q C M O E U
X J P P C S N I F U L K T M D O N V F
C O K M F T I P P X A N W S G E A O J
P U Q T E X M H S C U U Z O I K S U I
H P A R T H T M D M D H F B C M W S L
L V H O F D L M T E W Y Y T K N K W D
E C E E V A W T A E H C X H G U A U J
Y G W D B G X Z J B X H G N B F I D W
```

AUTUMN	_____	CLOUDY	_____
COLD	_____	DROUGHT	_____
DRY	_____	FOG	_____
HEAT WAVE	_____	HOT	_____
MIST	_____	OVERCAST	_____
RAIN	_____	RAINBOW	_____
SNOW	_____	SPRING	_____
STORM	_____	SUMMER	_____
SUNNY	_____	WET	_____
WINDY	_____	WINTER	_____

Numbers

```
K L S N A W B C T P S Z N K Q L V P X
E K K E F C J D F I N L R P R S U I B
V G Q E R J T Z X E X G N R F I S H J
L D H T X W I S E J X K R N W X I F Z
D W N E E X N T Y V M Q N J X T X V M
Y S H N K P R X G A L D N E V E L E P
L L T I V I Q A T W O E G N C E K F K
H Y G N H G T H G I E W W B R N G N U
U F D T H O K S D V Z G S T E Y I E C
P Q H F Y H J R E C F E W Y R D B E X
E O K D B V X E S O V R Q Y A M F T J
U M R R B X R V U E O U D U B F U H P
F I V E S H C R N N F O F C M V L G I
A R A A T T T E I O F E N I N G I X
H P N U E E E R E Y K W Z B S W R E C
D M C N E E W R T B Z N E V E S O O M
I D Z N N O U O F N Z D C L T S W R N
I Q F M C A E G I N Y Z I Z T N L D F
H O W O K V B R F E O V O R S D N M A
```

ONE	_____	TWO	_____
THREE	_____	FOUR	_____
FIVE	_____	SIX	_____
SEVEN	_____	EIGHT	_____
NINE	_____	TEN	_____
ELEVEN	_____	TWELVE	_____
THIRTEEN	_____	FOURTEEN	_____
FIFTEEN	_____	SIXTEEN	_____
SEVENTEEN	_____	EIGHTEEN	_____
NINETEEN	_____	TWENTY	_____

4

Colors

```
K U A H D E R M I X U L A I M R L F S
A L Q S C Z D Z K B V G W H I T E K N
X G K P E A I Z H U Z S P W J Q I D N
T Q N U R V C H F N T G F A E W L S O
N X I K E L Y Z E U C H G M W O Q H K
N G P M Q B Z G R E E N G M G B H U N
M F N B E I V I E G Q W X I R W A N S
V U F U I J Z X I M R B I O L X A R G
G Q L T V K P E X M B O N X P I E E Q
X B W T C N B Y X C G Z J U G C L V R
T M U A I Q H Y L Y E D R N J U S L E
B U L U B C E Y N K U P D B B Z U I C
L B R Q W R O J D E L E N I R K K S L
N X V Q G O N L A E G D Z R W O M J W
Z A H N U E L D O N N J K X R Q W N Y
L G V Y I O S L A R O A R M C V V N L
G H X Y A J I R E N E U K S M S X S K
Z J N B G U O S S Y O D S E B V T U F
I M Q V K N J F E X G K R Q Q P D D Q
```

BEIGE	_____	BLACK	_____
BLUE	_____	BRONZE	_____
BROWN	_____	DARK	_____
GOLD	_____	GREEN	_____
GREY	_____	LIGHT	_____
MULTICOLORED	_____	NAVY	_____
ORANGE	_____	PINK	_____
PURPLE	_____	RED	_____
SILVER	_____	TURQUOISE	_____
WHITE	_____	YELLOW	_____

Common Verbs 1

```
Y  X  O  U  C  I  J  M  N  X  I  Z  N  C  A  K  N  E  B
N  M  G  Z  Q  A  L  A  I  R  A  O  X  A  L  Y  B  H  Q
C  Z  I  X  N  E  S  K  E  Q  X  T  S  Q  A  B  I  M  J
Y  J  V  D  B  C  X  E  Q  K  G  V  Q  V  X  L  O  O  K
S  S  E  F  J  O  E  C  L  O  S  E  E  H  M  E  K  A  Y
Y  A  W  W  O  L  L  O  F  T  C  P  X  I  B  N  P  J  P
F  Y  N  M  M  L  Z  O  S  W  F  A  Q  Y  Y  L  X  D  C
A  K  W  V  I  Q  G  F  O  K  Y  N  R  A  E  L  I  O  L
R  N  H  K  F  Q  W  N  O  R  J  R  C  H  A  G  N  G  C
W  O  E  U  T  Z  K  O  C  P  K  R  C  S  I  F  W  K  F
G  X  F  G  F  Z  C  H  Y  U  B  N  G  M  Z  I  L  C  B
J  L  R  O  C  C  E  G  F  N  X  D  I  U  O  B  H  F  H
T  G  E  M  O  C  J  V  P  U  T  H  A  R  R  B  I  Y  N
V  D  G  P  L  M  L  P  A  F  K  X  N  L  D  K  T  Z  O
M  N  R  B  Q  F  P  Q  S  E  R  F  S  L  B  U  E  F  T
A  T  B  I  I  P  Q  E  Q  C  L  E  I  D  A  O  B  T  F
Q  R  U  N  V  T  N  M  O  F  O  P  E  N  I  S  L  A  G
Q  F  D  H  Y  E  S  O  R  U  A  C  H  F  T  G  K  E  P
G  D  E  U  O  N  D  M  K  B  X  L  G  G  F  G  V  K  D
```

ASK	_____	BUY	_____
CLOSE	_____	COME	_____
COOK	_____	DRINK	_____
DRIVE	_____	EAT	_____
FIND	_____	FOLLOW	_____
GIVE	_____	GO	_____
HELP	_____	KNOW	_____
LEARN	_____	LEAVE	_____
LIKE	_____	LOOK	_____
MAKE	_____	OPEN	_____

Solutions p. 68

Common Verbs 2

```
S N D G O K Y V V S F I Z R I L X Q X
I B D Q R G Q V G Z A X U L P L X H A
R V G O E E K W A N T Y V A S R T U Z
M E W B K R Z J G O V D E D W C S C I
E W A G A D Y I J D S A X Y U E I I Q
M H T D T P V P V B P X T M E A C K U
T F S H U A R Z W L E Y A L P E L A L
J A P Z T Y H U Y I A I V Y O A Z M N
Y Y H L J E M R N X K I W T W O Z X R
A S N C C J T X P Y Z E U D X D L Z F
N X T S B J K J C P U T U P N W P X Y
W L Z A V X C R K Q U M C P F S G E K
T G P W R I S F H T E L L F E O Y S X
I X V A X T Q R R W F L T E N Y M F V
L T Z I T U B E O Y G G L S J K C K O
A M G T E H B I U T H E T I R W R T A
N R S Q Z I Y I Q B C J S P E E L S F
H Q D J Z Y I U N D E R S T A N D G Z
P G P O U E F W Z G P P F O Z U U I T
```

PAY	_____	PLAY	_____
PUT	_____	READ	_____
RUN	_____	SAY	_____
SEE	_____	SLEEP	_____
SPEAK	_____	START	_____
TAKE	_____	TELL	_____
TRY	_____	UNDERSTAND	_____
USE	_____	WAIT	_____
WALK	_____	WANT	_____
WORK	_____	WRITE	_____

Preposition of place

```
B O U L M D F V H X T X O L T L D D H
H T F P G E B F S I X E R O K A W J O
N T O E S T G Y Y F M T T V B V A M I
S X T Y O E E H V J L I O E D P R K N
S E N Y J V B A Z X Y S L B B B N D S
K N O F W C E W E T S O K T G M W N I
R B R X L X L R P R W P R Q C I M X D
H L F L H V W O A M D P D N U O R A E
L W N G B Z A E S Q R O D K U N W M Y
R B I C M U N U V E P T P N N O P O K
U C S O B X B T I P T E I D D U W R I
K E D O Y T E S P H C O A S E T V F R
R U C T V C H V X Z X Y E D R S B R C
Z L X K I K I N C G O Z D O N I R A E
I D X E H C N G W L T P I S E D V F I
V T B P I L D D S C X K S M A E R G C
V X S L I Z X N G B D N E X T J X K G
B P N A B O V E W S O Z B Q H Z Y W M
E Z H C N E E W T E B Q Z U N D E R J
```

ABOVE	_____	AROUND	_____
AT	_____	BEHIND	_____
BELOW	_____	BESIDE	_____
BETWEEN	_____	CLOSE TO	_____
FAR FROM	_____	IN	_____
IN FRONT OF	_____	INSIDE	_____
NEAR	_____	NEXT TO	_____
ON	_____	OPPOSITE	_____
OUTSIDE	_____	OVER	_____
UNDER	_____	UNDERNEATH	_____

Solutions p. 68

Family

```
C R E T H G U A D D N A R G G J B H X
E E F I W T Q L Q X N E P H E W M O Z
P H J F S K P I U C O U S I N I H D X
A J T F N Q N Y Q S P O U S E B H G P
X W P A R E N T S E F J P O B M N A R
P N X Z E M V C F A Z R O P O G Z E M
O P X H H C G B T R E O I T G N H P S
Q S X V T S C H L H Y E H S R T K O J
D X A M O T E D T Q X E B H O W N H F
D Y Q K R R X A D H R C A M M H C S L
W K I S B A F F F N L F D Z G V I E M
Z R J H Q D M U M U A N X X B S P I U
X N F Y N U Z P V P A B L C T T K N F
Y U I A U N C L E R U X S E T M W N T
M Q R E H R S F G E N D R U F T M N F
F G Z C C W V A J L T T S O H U Y Y O
E M H O T E P A R E N T S I N L A W V
H B T U C Q U S S B N R E T H G U A D
T N O S D N A R G T T T H B Q R E A F
```

AUNT	_____	BROTHER	_____
COUSIN	_____	DAUGHTER	_____
FATHER	_____	GRANDDAUGHTER	_____
GRANDFATHER	_____	GRANDMOTHER	_____
GRANDSON	_____	HUSBAND	_____
MOTHER	_____	NEPHEW	_____
NIECE	_____	PARENTS	_____
PARENTS-IN-LAW	_____	SISTER	_____
SON	_____	SPOUSE	_____
UNCLE	_____	WIFE	_____

The head

```
W  X  J  B  K  R  Q  H  D  B  Y  X  P  Q  L  J  F  W  P
K  V  L  I  S  N  B  E  K  X  X  R  P  N  I  N  O  A  A
M  Q  W  C  H  O  D  X  L  U  F  R  I  N  P  S  R  V  R
A  R  L  X  W  K  G  G  D  M  W  L  T  A  S  Q  E  Q  N
J  T  O  F  A  C  E  X  R  G  R  D  A  E  H  K  H  E  K
R  B  N  O  S  T  R  I  L  L  R  P  W  O  G  Q  E  M  R
V  H  T  E  M  P  L  E  V  O  S  N  V  C  E  H  A  B  P
D  N  V  S  G  H  T  O  O  T  Q  M  U  J  H  Y  D  E  L
V  J  J  M  O  U  S  T  A  C  H  E  Z  I  C  E  E  W  R
K  L  S  J  T  V  H  S  G  I  R  K  Y  N  Y  Z  E  H  C
E  L  B  T  O  O  Z  T  S  Z  Q  S  V  E  I  P  N  K  D
E  Y  Q  T  N  R  S  T  U  C  S  E  A  N  L  H  K  W  M
J  M  T  E  G  Z  M  K  V  O  H  E  B  F  V  I  C  V  B
B  O  U  P  U  N  O  S  E  S  M  E  M  J  P  I  D  Y  T
W  O  R  B  E  Y  E  K  W  L  A  J  K  O  D  C  S  D  G
O  U  M  K  T  Y  G  F  O  R  Z  U  V  E  A  R  J  M  H
A  B  F  L  C  V  Y  C  D  O  K  J  D  B  H  C  Z  K  S
F  T  X  L  M  H  W  B  S  J  I  U  N  M  P  S  T  K  T
D  Q  J  J  W  A  S  E  H  S  A  L  E  Y  E  E  Y  G  V
```

BEARD	_____	CHEEK	_____
CHIN	_____	EAR	_____
EYE	_____	EYEBROW	_____
EYELASHES	_____	EYELID	_____
FACE	_____	FOREHEAD	_____
HAIR	_____	HEAD	_____
LIPS	_____	MOUSTACHE	_____
MOUTH	_____	NOSE	_____
NOSTRIL	_____	TEMPLE	_____
TONGUE	_____	TOOTH	_____

The body

```
E B L Y Z N E C K U R B G V M F U G U
B O H V D C N Y S T U B R H U D N J Y
I E S D K G E K Q N P V F E S Z H J S
R G N A E K H A A R M M P F H I E T V
J A X L N Z K C R X X K X L O A I H F
H R Z E T K A C H F V G B E U S R I J
D F E F M Y L Q L E W E I N L M A G E
A N M G O N T E N Q S J T T D U K H B
R S T R N M D W Y C K T G Y E N N T J
W W G D S I O F M C W E S J R C U M V
J R J U X B F R A G E P W A S D C L I
F I U S L P T B F L A C G P W Z C X D
Z S U E Y S N H C C I K D O Q V J O I
I T X I I Y N O F B N N A M P A A T J
Z N Y A X I D E D O M E S F L U A O Z
C E W G H O O A D F O E R N E F Z E C
L F Z S U L W P R E L T I E E O O H S
Q S X O S Z U S I V X B A C H A Z G K
Y D M E G W C Q C I E Y S T O M A C H
```

ANKLE	_____	ARM	_____
BACK	_____	CALF	_____
CHEST	_____	ELBOW	_____
FINGER	_____	FOOT	_____
HAND	_____	HEEL	_____
KNEE	_____	LEG	_____
NECK	_____	SHIN	_____
SHOULDER	_____	STOMACH	_____
THIGH	_____	TOE	_____
WAIST	_____	WRIST	_____

Physical Appearance

```
C A Q U X J B S Q G Q M A Y P G Z Q I
S M L N L Z M I U H K W Q K E S Z U D
L L E I H A V F P P Y W Y F S L M J G
K X N D L Y R I A H B N N K L O A U P
Z Y A L I S Q G G A V Q P R I U W U I
H K F A T U V T L Z A I R N M F R P W
O F W X V E M D R A L U C S U M I L Y
S U I G S L N F N E O U R O E E N U M
N M G T Y R T T O R X F C G L R K F M
L O N L R D G N C B T T S W J D L I T
Z R Z T Y I A N Z X D K C V D T E T V
T F B L D K P S U L G R P C E U D U V
H G A D L Y D X T O B I G P D Z V A W
L I N L S A Y L R A Y C O R R G J E N
Q G U O V C T K O U K F N E A S Q B K
E E U N R H H C H T H I N T E E R G P
X B G G B T P B S E O L S T B T T Q C
Z R K A I Z S V I G E X Y Y P E N M N
J F U S O M U K F H Q M Y G D Y W V F
```

BALD	_____	
BEAUTIFUL	_____	
FAT	_____	
LONG	_____	
OLD	_____	
SHORT	_____	
SMALL	_____	
TALL	_____	
UGLY	_____	
WRINKLED	_____	

BEARDED	_____	
BIG	_____	
HAIRY	_____	
MEDIUM	_____	
PRETTY	_____	
SLIM	_____	
STRONG	_____	
THIN	_____	
MUSCULAR	_____	
YOUNG	_____	

Solutions p. 69

Characters

```
I Y T S A N S C J T C S P J H R L A O
O W E Y Z U J Z P C B B Q X N H U A T
G E N E R O U S L E L N P Q N X P S L
F I L F R H V E H H N C Y H S X E S N
J I F F V E V J H C E O U F O N U E Z
H A M B U E Q J G Y Z A L R O T Q O F
N S N W R C P O L I T E B H I A Q L T
G A E V I T I S N E S N S H Q O S U N
U J O L Y N P Y F Q D I I E Z T U U E
Z K P R F S A B F D D O V C U Y J S I
Q X P F O I S N R L O I Y B E X A H T
D T Y Y Q E S O E A T J B T O A N W A
K W L R N J T H B C V O C I S F Q R P
R O L U H N F F A U R E Q A S E G D S
R A I I O A U K S N R D V R O O N E X
O Q S X I S S F H U N Q V F M Z K O Q
C B M R H I L H J Q U M Y K Z H Y X H
B K D G F A M X Z C O N Z P B I Z F G
P Q E U D F I I F W O F Z Z L C S P C
```

ACTIVE	_____	BOSSY	_____
BRAVE	_____	CLEVER	_____
CURIOUS	_____	DISHONEST	_____
FAIR	_____	FUNNY	_____
GENEROUS	_____	HONEST	_____
LAZY	_____	NASTY	_____
NICE	_____	PATIENT	_____
POLITE	_____	SELFISH	_____
SENSITIVE	_____	SHY	_____
SILLY	_____	STUBBORN	_____

Feelings 1

```
Z S C I N T E R E S T E D J J E A B E
D S D F G L A D Q Y M Z X H K I G D U
T J W T U Z Q I A E G C A L M L E L T
A H L Z P R J V S B X U X O U Z X Y R
D R C O N F I D E N T H H Z A E D V H
C W E Z X T J O D I N R A M L B I V U
D B Q E C J X P U A A U A U A Z Q E V
G D E E P T U C O S D F U S S N J G M
G I M V K G D H H B E R G I T G H Z
W S B O R E D F H W O Y P A M L E R Q
I A A P D B W L U I K P J R I Z Z D Y
M P R E C A U T I O U S E X E D C P G
P P R D I S G U S T E D R L V S D W X
R O A I F R I G H T E N E D E Q S D F
E I S T C L S V M S D Q V Y Y S V E R
S N S K G S G U F P T E P K A E S O D
S T E X C I T E D K H P M Z J N E O M
E E D S G A M P R I A M F P R O J C Y
D D U G Q X A M T H D Q C Z X M S X E
```

AFRAID	_____	AMAZED	_____
ANGRY	_____	BORED	_____
CALM	_____	CAUTIOUS	_____
CONFIDENT	_____	DEPRESSED	_____
DISAPPOINTED	_____	DISGUSTED	_____
EMBARRASSED	_____	EXCITED	_____
EXHAUSTED	_____	FRIGHTENED	_____
FURIOUS	_____	GLAD	_____
HAPPY	_____	HOPELESS	_____
IMPRESSED	_____	INTERESTED	_____

Feelings 2

```
O U T Q E T K S H O C K E D E X D H T
P F W W S U R P R I S E D P V S V D Y
H B P F T S X D T J N C R I N Z G S S
D L I P H Q U T Y N L O I V E Z H C U
H L L E W N R C Q C U Z L Q V Z W Q O
Y Q J R H Q K D S D G T A F I S M L L
A R U A O P X H I D G X V I S J U I A
P A P E F S U O V R E N F O N O Z A E
A P O D T R J D T N G R L Q E Y D B J
Y L K A E V I B E S C W I T P F E K B
U D H A H X O S Q R S Y U T S U S M Z
G N M V E R A B T Z E B P P Q L S A D
Z N Q Q O W D L U U J I L R S Y E D G
Z Z T E E Q S E E W B H E O D E R A K
V V L W S B I O R R E U A M Q O T Q N
D W H K C I S O T A J E S J O E S B N
D E I R R O W P Q K C E E R G V N V A
O C N F T T F A F V N S D G Z S P G V
Q R R O D E I F S I T A S W S X Z V N
```

JEALOUS	_____	JOYFUL	_____
NERVOUS	_____	PENSIVE	_____
PLEASED	_____	PROUD	_____
RELAXED	_____	SAD	_____
SATISFIED	_____	SCARED	_____
SHOCKED	_____	SICK	_____
STRESSED	_____	SURPRISED	_____
TIRED	_____	UNHAPPY	_____
UPSET	_____	WEAK	_____
WELL	_____	WORRIED	_____

Restaurant

```
M E D I U M R A R E B D P W O T E A Q
W R L R O T A K E A W A Y M Y E Z E B
I G J A D F G S B G E J J C Q J E F E
N A I L Y R R N P J F M I M U R H W C
O B B L J I O N G V C P U Y Y B Z E H
T W I G I E R Y P U S E M R G T P L F
T E L D W S A N I J I D E E A D E L C
L I L Z D H R T F G K V R M A W P D E
C K P G A L E B L Z I C T I V L P O Q
X B D H N L M S V L W T X C N S E N N
F R Z L L O C L E N G X Q C N K R E C
R M W I Z Y R D A F U S H I S M L L M
Y C R M T V R D O D L D D E S S E R T
S G V F D Q L X E J J E Y I B W O N G
A Z V Q E P A D W R V B P O V D M L U
U Y L M H N R S E L G O K U X Z V M D
C Z K F O Z D S A U M L C H I P S N X
E O H F Z A K U A L W D A P I U W S K
X F K L P S J S X S T R A W I V A X I
```

BILL	_____	CHIPS	_____
DELIVERY	_____	DESSERT	_____
DRINK	_____	FRIES	_____
GRILL	_____	MEAL	_____
MEDIUM RARE	_____	MENU	_____
ORDER	_____	PEPPER	_____
RARE	_____	SALT	_____
SAUCE	_____	SPICY	_____
STRAW	_____	TAKE AWAY	_____
TIP	_____	WELL-DONE	_____

Solutions p. 70

Food

```
D  S  C  D  M  V  Y  S  P  I  C  H  O  C  X  A  Y  Z  W
D  M  Y  Z  O  J  T  I  U  C  S  I  B  W  Y  R  G  S  O
Q  A  V  T  U  O  X  U  M  S  E  O  A  O  X  F  S  G  X
E  E  K  J  M  F  F  W  H  A  T  W  R  N  Z  K  H  U  E
N  R  L  Y  A  G  M  A  Q  E  J  T  U  E  X  P  P  E  I
D  C  I  W  P  I  M  I  E  V  O  M  N  M  K  K  M  F  R
I  E  M  W  F  U  D  C  O  S  C  J  S  D  D  A  P  Y  W
L  C  W  E  Z  U  A  A  P  D  A  Q  Y  A  L  I  C  M  X
R  I  A  W  C  U  Y  G  E  A  N  I  I  A  U  E  E  D  H
F  S  Q  Z  E  O  F  Y  S  R  M  U  E  B  R  S  B  S  C
S  I  W  O  G  M  P  K  S  F  B  R  L  T  U  N  A  K  S
P  O  S  U  A  O  H  A  W  G  E  Z  J  T  T  W  V  G  C
Q  P  R  H  W  E  D  X  S  C  E  M  U  W  I  R  Q  V  E
Y  T  C  N  S  M  V  B  G  T  T  C  S  D  E  V  E  J  S
I  D  A  E  B  H  O  T  Y  E  A  R  I  T  Y  A  O  V  Q
V  Q  E  E  X  H  V  T  Y  Y  Y  L  T  R  A  D  P  D  P
W  H  J  M  M  M  A  H  M  E  T  U  O  E  T  R  D  P  Q
C  W  M  R  R  B  M  H  R  Q  B  P  P  S  Z  R  G  Y  O
J  C  L  O  L  K  X  U  S  A  N  D  W  I  C  H  Z  G  M
```

BISCUIT	_____	BREAD	_____
BUTTER	_____	CAKE	_____
CEREAL	_____	CHEESE	_____
EGG	_____	FISH	_____
HAM	_____	ICE CREAM	_____
JAM	_____	MEAT	_____
MILK	_____	PASTA	_____
RICE	_____	SANDWICH	_____
SAUSAGE	_____	SEAFOOD	_____
TUNA	_____	YOGURT	_____

Fruits 1

```
V S U V A E H A T F Q O D Y C F N J I
L G R A P E F R U I T D X S B S Z W A
X W X A F R E S H F R U I T D M L F W
V F R U I T S A L A D N T Z N I X V U
J G H P V V B X M P C E B B A E K H O
B L A C K B E R R Y N S A E S P D L E
W F M W K A D L Y I M T N S O Y P C M
C O C O N U T Z T B I C A B M M I L X
N Q X N P C X N X U S E N C U U C Z E
M B L B I C E R F O B A U J A K Y M
H R L L V M B F H D U S O T U U R R R
J M C U E W D R A E U I I K G O U Z T
F F H L E E P C L R R U N I W F X O K
V W C B I B O X T C R R F W Z Q C J Q
D T R R F V E I Y F V G Y I Q I B X E
D A D Y A E C R Q K N H N P R Q H F D
L P T O Z B Y T R M I P M P Z S A I P
O Q K E N U O N F Y S O A P V R W I U
R N J E T O O F R U I T T R E E D M N
```

APPLE	_____	APRICOT	_____
AVOCADO	_____	BANANA	_____
BLACKBERRY	_____	BLUEBERRY	_____
CHERRY	_____	CITRUS	_____
CLEMENTINE	_____	COCONUT	_____
DATE	_____	DRIED FRUIT	_____
FIG	_____	FRESH FRUIT	_____
FRUIT JUICE	_____	FRUIT SALAD	_____
FRUIT TREE	_____	GRAPE	_____
GRAPEFRUIT	_____	KIWI	_____

Solutions p. 71

Fruits 2

```
Q P G E V K V I S C H V E V J E U S G
W I C X T I U R F N O I S S A P J Y N
O P P S N Q K I F X R X O R A N G E S
A J B C O F N P N O M M I S R E P M K
V M V D L A Z G E N I R A T C E N H E
S Z A E E L L Y C H E E L X N P Y Y R
Y U F N M P V V J D U G I O C I U R X
K S B V D F K I P P I U M L N N X R L
Y M G L B A P B Y Y L W E O Z E M E J
R K R N V T R S Y L N U L J V A A B Y
R B X J Z K C I H N M E M Z V P P P L
E C Y R H B A L N J M Z S N F P X S D
B O S S W Y U D F R S C O R F L J A P
W N H H A K P Q E V M M F A Z E O R H
A A X P F E R T O M E E F E F G A V C
R A A F A B A W J L S X R P N E J Y C
T P A C R W A V V H P N R A W C X O I
S D H D G W D B K T I K M V F W Q L I
Z E T A N A R G E M O P X L F R D Q E
```

LEMON	_____	LIME	_____
LYCHEE	_____	MANDARIN	_____
MANGO	_____	MELON	_____
NECTARINE	_____	ORANGE	_____
PAPAYA	_____	PASSION FRUIT	_____
PEACH	_____	PEAR	_____
PERSIMMON	_____	PINEAPPLE	_____
PIP	_____	PLUM	_____
POMEGRANATE	_____	RASPBERRY	_____
STRAWBERRY	_____	WATERMELON	_____

Vegetables 1

```
K V H R F Q A E G G P L A N T E K B A
R B D Z N R I K G E Y C Z P R R Q E B
G M W E O W J L S H N D Z M L G M E S
H C H P D Y M T Y Q E D Y V H A O T Z
N U N A F G R B E P F R I W L S E R B
H C Y L L O K M I S U D K V L P R O R
O U Y N N X D F I M P Z R I E A B O U
X M B F X S Z C H I V E S T N R R T S
L B C E Z G C A B M W E T W Q A O Z S
D E O C A R R O T O T C Y T Q G C J E
A R R K V N B Y L T R R A M N U C B L
R A N Q S K R F E Z C D H B J S O V S
T A I L H E I G E G M H P B B G L X S
I Q A F L L R F Q L A N I P G A I P P
C D X E U U X C B Y Q R W L W I G M R
H I C A O O J X R A E C L R L Y C E O
O W C C B G I A Q K K A R I I I H Z U
K P P S I O A C G N A P V D C C H E T
E C Z E J F C H E R R Y T O M A T O T
```

ARTICHOKE	_____	ASPARAGUS	_____
BEAN	_____	BEETROOT	_____
BROCCOLI	_____	BRUSSELS SPROUT	_____
CABBAGE	_____	CARROT	_____
CAULIFLOWER	_____	CELERY	_____
CHERRY TOMATO	_____	CHILLI	_____
CHIVES	_____	CORN	_____
COURGETTE	_____	CUCUMBER	_____
EGGPLANT	_____	ENDIVE	_____
GARLIC	_____	GHERKIN	_____

Solutions p. 71

Vegetables 2

```
Z L A E U N P D Z E E A D F E Z Z C Z
C O F J R E I H T H X W C A Y O S P N
O R J S P P P B R A B U H R P H D I G
G O X P Z Q O G C I W T W D C C N K U
U D E U J H H V I G T Q I A M K L P V
Q R Z P S I U I P N Y J N I O X D D G
A O S L H S H B V C G I T B P E A P V
H W W C P I N R U T P E T Y F L E E K
X Z V R N W U O A S B U R A Y E X G C
M R O O N I O N T D T I O A G T H S Z
M U S H R O O M O A I I R F P T F M M
D A W M Z X M B K I T S U E Z U J G S
O T A M O T I Z A Y N O H M Q C I E H
N S U S W D K S B P A M P X W E G A K
Z G R J V Y C L Z A V S H A L L O T I
E C I N A G R O V G F H S A U Q S C M
C Y R P U M P K I N W K U I U Z W W R
V O O T A T O P T E E W S C I Y K T M
W I T N S L I T N E L K D T B H U C U
```

GINGER	_____	LEEK	_____
LENTILS	_____	LETTUCE	_____
MUSHROOM	_____	ONION	_____
ORGANIC	_____	PEA	_____
PEPPER	_____	POTATO	_____
PUMPKIN	_____	RADISH	_____
RHUBARB	_____	SHALLOT	_____
SOYA	_____	SPINACH	_____
SQUASH	_____	SWEET POTATO	_____
TOMATO	_____	TURNIP	_____

Pets & Farm animals

```
O C L J V L D P N Y H V E T T D D Y P
B A G K G O L D F I S H O Q E K V Q J
K A F P E E H S K T X B F Q F R O G U
D Z A L N Z U F N T A O G D P R H W R
U P U I B P Y K P T T G O W E X D G E
T T E J A M V D N N U G P A I U V L A
Q M G D N E S R O H R R L D Q H J M C
S E O I O U O R Q Y T N K L P O N Y A
L A W U T L K N E Y L P Q E O N B J N
G F C X S R H K H L E H X I Y K R G Q
V P N U A E N M F A P D G L X X C G L
C N G B N O L G C A J L U N O L L O G
B V B B D A Q A R A A T E C J T Q H C
X I M G D A T R P C O K V Q K L R O W
T G L E O V O F O F C P C Y B Z B S R
W L Y A O T N W Q I I F A S R Z Y O D
H C G W P Z X D H G G V G Z Z G A Y K
U W L K H M L C H A M S T E R H O O Q
O P H X P T L F G B A N L T P U O D G
```

CAT	_____	CHICKEN	_____
COCK	_____	COW	_____
DOG	_____	DONKEY	_____
DUCK	_____	FROG	_____
GOAT	_____	GOLDFISH	_____
HAMSTER	_____	HORSE	_____
MOUSE	_____	PARROT	_____
PIG	_____	PONY	_____
RABBIT	_____	SHEEP	_____
TURKEY	_____	TURTLE	_____

Solutions p. 72

Wild animals

```
S N X M I A J R A E P Y K Z C P E O S
Z N Y F N L C G C O T X P N S T J X N
Q G F L J L U A A Q O J K O W G A K M
O B U X Q I Q H M G H L Z G P M O O U
F T A B R O B C E M W W H Q F A W F K
T M Y A H N O M L J S Y L M L J Z L G
W T M U T P W T L B L A G A V C L E O
Z N O W Z O W L E K A N S L R W X C R
Y A N R B G I R A F F E K O E W S K I
U H K H E R H A L R G H C D H Q A B L
M P E I A Y S Y D C B O J Z Z N S A L
H E Y N R V Z Q P N D P W Q G S B A A
V L S O F N E A I A O U A M Y V J X
A E U C M U B A L E L P R J K A M B V
O X I E U Y R E C F J O J S P D W X D
M I R R Y J A F A W O R Z V M K G E V
U F V O W V U M O W K I P Y L O I J E
J B P S Q F J D U X T I G E R U Z P L
Y X K F H I P P O P O T A M U S N W V
```

BAT	_____	BEAR	_____
CAMEL	_____	CROCODILE	_____
ELEPHANT	_____	FOX	_____
GIRAFFE	_____	GORILLA	_____
HIPPOPOTAMUS	_____	KANGAROO	_____
KOALA	_____	LION	_____
MONKEY	_____	OWL	_____
PANDA	_____	RHINOCEROS	_____
SNAKE	_____	TIGER	_____
WOLF	_____	ZEBRA	_____

Insects

```
Q C F M R O W F O K L C R E D I P S U
N L X L T J Y L F N O G A R D J B Q Y
H P L A D Y B I R D T N T G K E M H U
J D C A T E R P I L L A R D M M Q D X
W V H Z T B W A S P D A N T O I T J W
I V Z B U T T E R F L Y U J W D N M Z
K H Y M V M O S Q U I T O J I A C C U
V T O D E A B G Z S U Z V O J O Z G F
Z K E R Q D Z Y Z B Y C R E C P R L P
L D C K N S D I S M E K T K J A D Z X
R L L M C E K N F Q S E R J S S P F G
F P M A M I T A L Q N O L S T G E Q X
B H M D S D R J E F A V H C L T Z H C
E L Z A B D N C A C L O U I E C K B N
C U S C J L O X H S P Y C R R X E X H
C O T I P K T Z G P U E M N O E B O F
I C B C C D Y X E P R I G X T Y M M M
E Q T E X S F R E P T J H L D X W A U
J T S Z Y V E Y M E A V E B Z Y E G T
```

ANT	_____	BEE	_____
BEETLE	_____	BUTTERFLY	_____
CATERPILLAR	_____	CICADA	_____
COCKROACH	_____	CRICKET	_____
DRAGONFLY	_____	FLEA	_____
FLY	_____	GRASSHOPPER	_____
HORNET	_____	LADYBIRD	_____
LICE	_____	MOSQUITO	_____
SPIDER	_____	TERMITE	_____
WASP	_____	WORM	_____

Solutions p. 72

Hobbies

```
K F C M O G S A I Q A N M R A G L Z M
T Y H P A R G O T O H P G N I L I A S
V Q N E D S U F Y P O T T E R Y E P D
M U S G S E Y I K L A W A C R Q F R J
R J B U F W W S R X L S L E T C N G P
P E B Q R I J H J H C O A J P P N E F
E Z S G N O I Y G R D D J X I S P G
T Y X X A G M N W N I R L X P D A B N
T G K P Q R A G J N A K O M L A L O I
N A N A R B D G G W H E A C F H B K L
D W S I O T N E I X I C D G H Q R G E
K F C N K I R N N U K N G T N D G U V
A D L T K O G M S I I L A L O I M X A
Y U R I U O O N M A N N I Z Q B M D R
G R B N B Y J C I X G G N I V I D A T
Y J W G M F D H A D D Z U V W S C U G
C Y T M V A F Z E R I B Y I D U G G Y
I E Q D K N G J I P Z R H U N T I N G
W H P R T U B P C O V P J U D W J R U
```

BIKING	_____	CAMPING	_____
COOKING	_____	DIVING	_____
DIY	_____	DRAWING	_____
FISHING	_____	GAMING	_____
GARDENING	_____	HIKING	_____
HUNTING	_____	PAINTING	_____
PHOTOGRAPHY	_____	POTTERY	_____
READING	_____	RIDING	_____
SAILING	_____	SEWING	_____
TRAVELING	_____	WALK	_____

Jobs 1

```
O P N H R U T S I L A N R U O J G P E
Y G B O Z Q K K R H Z H S Z B A J V K
R N M H H H F G O E Y O Y G K R F W C
E W A Q O A K J A O V W D T W C D Z N
Y N W M C T R R D R C I M A K H F R I
A B H V R O S R N W D U R A J I D E Z
L T K N T E K V N Z D E C D R T R S K
K G C C M H I C P E T N E T E G S I
C X O W R E B S N N O N F E O C F E W
I D G R O C E R I R T I Z X R T P R C
R F S D K S D G Y F G T N F C P Y D S
B E B A R E N K C H A E I J G D K R Q
L Y Q E N E K W T D Q W Y R A N F I C
N H K T V A J E R K S D D E V G V A G
H A I R V Z R L Q W V F H M V R X H N
B S D D J E W E L L E R P R J J C E R
T J S B E L E C T R I C I A N K U A O
B A T U A N O R T S A H V F E V L T U
Z P A S P H R A C C O U N T A N T P P
```

ACCOUNTANT	_____	ACTOR	_____
ARCHITECT	_____	ASTRONAUT	_____
BAKER	_____	BRICKLAYER	_____
COOK	_____	DENTIST	_____
DOCTOR	_____	DRIVER	_____
ELECTRICIAN	_____	ENGINEER	_____
FARMER	_____	FIREFIGHTER	_____
FISHERMAN	_____	GARDENER	_____
GROCER	_____	HAIRDRESSER	_____
JEWELLER	_____	JOURNALIST	_____

Jobs 2

```
P V P H O T O G R A P H E R V F F T O
J K M E C H A N I C C R R Z V H N I Y
Y P K G Z J H P F M M U S I C I A N L
R F W E Y A O S I N G E R E T I A W B
A C Y W H S E A C N V Q A W E J P L D
T N V E T T O L I P R E X I E X O P O
E I B M P O H K E E K R T V W I O A U
R T A P D O U W T Z F C E X N Z Q I D
C N M X S J L I F H O M Y G L B F N Z
E B B L N S R I X N U R S E A D P T T
S D R D M W E X C Z F Q U Z W N C E S
O D W E C B U D S E L L E R Y C A R I
G M Q H B T K D R R O X G V E E P M C
S S G W G M C M M A V F Z Q R I Q Y A
V C C O P U U J P E W B F G Y E S F M
K Y F R R V M L P N G E Y I G O S A R
T V E S Y J G X P G X L T D C Z O R A
N Y V H U Y X Q A N O P U S N E B M H
N R V X E Y I M C A M J H K E Y R N P
```

JUDGE	_____	LAWYER	_____
MANAGER	_____	MECHANIC	_____
MUSICIAN	_____	NURSE	_____
PAINTER	_____	PHARMACIST	_____
PHOTOGRAPHER	_____	PILOT	_____
PLUMBER	_____	POLICE OFFICER	_____
POSTMAN	_____	SECRETARY	_____
SELLER	_____	SINGER	_____
STEWARDESS	_____	VET	_____
WAITER	_____	WRITER	_____

The classroom 1

```
W  H  I  G  H  L  I  G  H  T  E  R  C  S  K  W  N  M  B
U  C  Q  O  C  L  C  B  D  T  Q  O  Q  C  T  M  G  Z  X
U  T  N  Q  H  B  M  F  V  D  P  N  O  I  H  S  H  B  H
K  Q  S  K  A  D  H  A  X  Z  N  L  A  V  C  I  O  Q  Y
Q  H  L  O  I  G  Z  P  P  J  C  O  U  O  Q  O  S  Q  X
T  E  I  O  R  L  C  T  E  D  T  T  M  B  K  L  A  H  C
V  U  C  B  O  U  Z  Y  M  N  W  P  A  C  B  P  M  B  D
N  Q  N  E  T  E  K  K  O  P  U  N  A  N  B  Z  Y  E  M
D  B  E  T  A  D  O  A  Y  T  L  S  Q  R  I  W  Y  L  F
M  K  P  O  L  R  O  Q  E  D  E  B  R  E  N  U  H  I  G
U  N  D  N  U  A  B  R  Z  A  W  Y  O  S  K  U  D  F  O
B  M  E  A  C  O  F  D  B  Q  U  T  R  A  Y  E  Y  T  V
R  S  R  T  L  B  M  E  S  U  M  E  E  R  E  M  N  D  V
H  S  O  T  A  K  Q  S  V  G  K  R  J  E  D  I  B  Q  H
J  A  L  G  C  C  W  K  F  R  W  T  O  T  A  D  R  T  I
K  P  O  B  G  A  D  I  A  N  V  H  K  P  M  Q  U  D  B
B  M  C  I  V  L  R  M  Y  L  P  O  P  V  T  R  G  E  J
S  O  F  E  J  B  T  L  L  N  P  L  L  J  R  M  T  C  T
L  C  M  D  N  G  M  D  S  U  A  Y  O  Y  O  D  U  G  J
```

BIN	_____	BLACKBOARD	_____
BOOK	_____	BOOKCASE	_____
CALCULATOR	_____	CHAIR	_____
CHALK	_____	CLOCK	_____
COMPASS	_____	COMPUTER	_____
COLORED PENCILS	_____	DESK	_____
ERASER	_____	FILE	_____
GLUE	_____	HIGHLIGHTER	_____
MAP	_____	MARKER	_____
NOTEBOOK	_____	PAINT	_____

The classroom 2

```
V  E  Y  R  D  Q  W  E  S  A  C  L  I  C  N  E  P  N  O
N  T  Z  S  L  F  P  E  N  G  Y  X  T  Z  W  L  C  X  Y
L  R  H  I  R  U  K  T  E  A  C  H  E  R  C  Z  L  R  Q
E  E  W  L  Z  U  H  U  D  O  E  D  E  X  U  B  J  H  P
S  N  O  X  I  L  B  N  Z  T  X  L  L  L  P  U  T  B  A
C  E  D  T  O  T  T  B  A  I  W  E  B  E  I  A  V  N  I
H  P  A  E  P  E  Z  L  E  R  L  A  A  S  N  P  T  P  N
O  R  W  E  E  S  K  S  R  D  L  T  E  A  A  R  K  T
O  A  M  H  W  D  N  T  L  K  F  Z  E  P  P  O  B  F  B
L  H  S  N  F  J  U  C  Y  H  O  K  E  E  J  Z  E  B  R
B  S  Q  T  S  D  A  O  I  D  R  R  D  E  R  A  H  K  U
A  L  K  E  E  C  P  J  I  L  C  K  C  N  E  V  C  O  S
G  I  I  N  Y  F  I  V  J  L  T  T  R  T  D  S  I  A  H
K  C  T  P  C  B  N  S  I  B  O  X  E  S  X  M  H  W  O
L  N  V  W  A  N  B  P  S  R  K  F  L  G  R  E  J  D  P
J  E  A  Y  Z  S  C  M  D  O  X  Z  P  S  U  Z  P  O  L
F  P  V  M  D  P  W  A  C  I  R  L  A  Q  L  W  B  O  E
P  R  O  T  R  A  C  T  O  R  K  S  T  C  E  F  A  S  M
U  D  B  G  H  E  U  Q  K  X  H  J  S  C  R  S  G  Y  I
```

PAINTBRUSH	_____	PAPER CLIP	_____
PEN	_____	PENCIL	_____
PENCIL CASE	_____	PENCIL SHARPENER	_____
PIN	_____	PROJECTOR	_____
PROTRACTOR	_____	RUBBER	_____
RULER	_____	SCHOOLBAG	_____
SCISSORS	_____	SHEET	_____
SLATE	_____	STAPLER	_____
STUDENT	_____	TABLE	_____
TAPE	_____	TEACHER	_____

Exam

```
Y A D E Q U B O M O E L I A F S X O B
Q C A Q S A E Q E K A T S I M N E R B
L Q N V C N V H W Y C M E M O R I Z E
S I V Y H I Q U B X Z W R O N G S W Q
M Q I N S T R U C T I O N S V E I Z R
N P D X T D B D L E X A M I N E R X S
D C C D R Y J U Y S A E I Z R H T B S
I Z V Z U N Z R E W S N A I W C A W K
F U L C E S A Q B L W J A K X Y E P X
F O B B S G D L P F F X Z H T F H B C
I C E E B R C Y G S E Y X X U C H D
C L U L S Y A V D N A S L P G S S S U
U G K B W Z E I H S O T L W B M S K J
L S K B X Z D I S N G I R A R L W A Q
T Z G J G Y A E S G D Y T M F X G C P
L F V H Y E R O P P Q H C S A G C V P
T Y K R D W G R V D Z C L U E E O D X
O E S I V E R M B P H C T A M U C U R
W M U L T I P L E C H O I C E W Q F A
```

ANSWER	_____	CHEAT	_____
DIFFICULT	_____	EASY	_____
ESSAY	_____	EXAMINER	_____
FAIL	_____	FALSE	_____
GRADE	_____	GUESS	_____
INSTRUCTIONS	_____	MATCH	_____
MEMORIZE	_____	MISTAKE	_____
MULTIPLE CHOICE	_____	PASS	_____
QUESTION	_____	REVISE	_____
TRUE	_____	WRONG	_____

Shopping

```
F O E L P O S D T X R E W G C E R R J
A I P N M U J E H E A O U Q F U J E P
H O G L S H K K J C X B C Z J U H F L
A A M D T S Z W U Q H P X F D S T U P
B C C T A D F H S I Q E E H P F I N J
T S A B W Z P N S A F Y A N P Y T D X
D K H S X W F Z C Y R P M P S U N K R
R K H E H D V H M Y P O O K O I O D E
I C O H L I Y V C R O J E K A F V A C
F G S F F F E P U R S E C G E O K E E
Q A L N S S L R G C U E R P H F P H I
C S B H V F D N A J H A X X S Q T L P
A Q U E U E I T S C B H T O S A L N T
N F Y N T T D O V X T K F H N I L N C
G J Z B T X U M C A Z Z D B T E F E W
L G Q I T R O L L E Y A H M H F P E E
U Y F Y K D W A L L E T H R B U S H Z
J Z Z K R R D T R C U S T O M E R V T
P Q E N S H O P A S S I S T A N T Z J
```

BAG	_____	BARGAIN	_____
BASKET	_____	CASH	_____
CASHIER	_____	CHEAP	_____
CHECK OUT	_____	CUSTOMER	_____
EXPENSIVE	_____	FITTING ROOM	_____
PURSE	_____	QUEUE	_____
RECEIPT	_____	REFUND	_____
SALE	_____	SHELF	_____
SHOP ASSISTANT	_____	TILL	_____
TROLLEY	_____	WALLET	_____

Clothes 1

```
C D L T P T P R A I N C O A T Z T F J
P O W A D E J X Y P M R T B Y X N R P
O O C G V C G I V L J J P Z E P L G A
O K J H C T X B Y D S H I R T L O X C
L Y J G V J K A D S T F F V R T T J S
Y C T U F I R K N I C K E R S M L T F
C O A T M B W K O Q O K B I B U A H H
X U H R O P D X A X G T O Z F H E G B
H S H D J J E A N S O S O J S F Y O J
P S C A R F M R Y X S A T U O C E B N
X N C A R D I G A N D N S H M V V Y Q
H R D Q U P V Q O I Z D F S L F U P Z
S W T D N X A W L D N A A N K Z J W B
U L V I B V K F T R Q L A Z X M A G W
L G L O V E S A L E P A N T S T C N G
E F H P Y J A M A S X L F N W F K N G
L W S R I M K O R S N U H E X S E Q V
J E A H N C M J D Q X Y B J S J T P B
I B X D C P A F L I P F L O P S C O G
```

BELT	_____	BOOTS	_____
BRA	_____	CAP	_____
CARDIGAN	_____	COAT	_____
DRESS	_____	FLIP-FLOPS	_____
GLOVES	_____	HAT	_____
JACKET	_____	JEANS	_____
JUMPER	_____	KNICKERS	_____
PANTS	_____	PYJAMAS	_____
RAINCOAT	_____	SANDAL	_____
SCARF	_____	SHIRT	_____

Solutions p. 74

Clothes 2

```
J O K L S K N E W O W S L P C Y J M U
S J U M U U I S M W O V K J W Z A R S
R H G R Z S R A Q N C V L I Y I O G T
Y K O H U E D Z S O C K S R R O N P O
I I S E S T Q A M L R F E H V T M A C
J I I U S U H T E S I V H A T T M T K
U D O L X T N K R S W P F E F D P B I
I R T X P C T D T A E E P P K E F T N
T I Y N F R Z R E H C G A E P V X A G
T N L H U Q O O K R K K T T R D X N S
R S C T X H O Y S M W S S I E S D K D
A H N T S X R Q O W M E N U G R Z T J
I N Q E H H K U Y B I A A Z I H Y O N
N Y R I A X U T E T Y M P R I T T P X
E W T Q Q K O E H G S Q S T R H T S Y
R C R K B H E Y P O D H W U M F I E E
S F S U I T B R Z F O T I V I B I D U
M M A S O O V E S T Z A R R K T E O Q
E O H L W I I U N I F O R M T X N K L
```

SHOES	_____	SHORTS	_____
SKIRT	_____	SLIPPERS	_____
SNEAKERS	_____	SOCKS	_____
STOCKINGS	_____	SUIT	_____
SWEATER	_____	SWIMSUIT	_____
T-SHIRT	_____	TANK TOP	_____
TIE	_____	TIGHTS	_____
TRACKSUIT	_____	TRAINERS	_____
TROUSERS	_____	UNDERWEAR	_____
UNIFORM	_____	VEST	_____

Nature

```
S  R  J  H  U  M  A  N  B  E  I  N  G  S  U  O  D  L  V
K  D  K  O  L  H  L  N  V  L  O  P  A  D  S  T  G  F  M
O  B  X  T  T  T  R  N  L  Q  O  D  M  K  D  N  I  W  T
V  S  H  E  P  R  Z  U  J  U  G  P  K  W  R  E  U  M  M
D  Y  P  U  X  A  G  Q  X  C  T  K  M  E  D  C  J  O  O
N  L  L  C  C  E  T  R  E  E  K  X  W  W  R  F  P  T  P
A  O  A  F  C  L  S  F  R  L  P  O  W  Y  N  U  R  W  H
S  S  B  E  S  A  O  P  V  X  L  P  Z  Z  K  I  G  M  Y
A  W  G  U  E  J  V  U  I  F  R  X  K  R  R  S  O  K  Q
B  O  T  I  C  T  W  D  Q  Y  H  N  E  N  O  V  D  A
B  X  T  L  S  S  I  C  Q  L  U  Q  U  R  N  N  O  L  C
T  K  C  I  O  M  W  B  Z  B  A  D  S  V  T  J  E  L  T
K  S  R  A  T  S  M  Y  E  S  R  C  M  T  Y  A  B  C  I
K  Q  A  S  G  Y  U  K  X  C  Q  F  M  J  F  S  K  D  P
V  L  N  D  W  A  T  E  R  H  E  R  I  F  G  L  J  L  A
R  L  R  S  A  N  Y  S  P  B  L  Q  S  L  L  I  A  F  A
T  X  I  C  I  Z  B  W  H  P  U  U  Z  I  N  N  A  R  Q
U  S  M  Z  R  R  S  S  A  R  G  E  N  O  T  S  D  U  N
K  J  U  J  D  U  J  D  O  O  W  V  X  Y  V  X  I  D  E
```

AIR	_____	CLOUD	_____
EARTH	_____	FIRE	_____
FLOWER	_____	GRASS	_____
HUMAN BEING	_____	ICE	_____
LEAF	_____	MOON	_____
PLANT	_____	SAND	_____
SKY	_____	STARS	_____
STONE	_____	SUN	_____
TREE	_____	WATER	_____
WIND	_____	WOOD	_____

Landscape

```
O Y E V A C Q A B O Q S C A P U K V Q
X O J Y A L R X P I P V N Y R C W C X
M E D I S Y R T N U O C Y A K I J U F
D J M A L M D E S E R T T T E Y V F V
H T U U C D B J I M L H N C I C H E C
R O Z N V F F I L C A D J D U C O U R
R B S M G X N I V Q H R N D M T M P G
W A L C W L O U A K E A F O S A S S T
N X O I F D E C I E L O U E E G A N L
U H T T P O K S F S O N R S B J M A A
N E B O D O W T I H T O Q W O I K U B
I T W J L L N R D A F S Z N K E N Z H
D F T D R F B X I L R B J H Y H T T A
C M F Q F E L N X H E C D V U A M J W
M L Y I C B M Q W O H I Z N X W N N V
G V A L L E Y Q H V I F F J O B S C T
Q V H V O L C A N O L A Z R D P T W Y
Q S Z I F L F M U F L F B Q W A U M I
T W A T E R F A L L Y P Y M N Z R Y A
```

CAVE	_____	CITY	_____
CLIFF	_____	COUNTRYSIDE	_____
DESERT	_____	FIELD	_____
FLOOD	_____	FOREST	_____
HILL	_____	ISLAND	_____
JUNGLE	_____	LAKE	_____
MOUNTAIN	_____	OCEAN	_____
POND	_____	RIVER	_____
SEA	_____	VALLEY	_____
VOLCANO	_____	WATERFALL	_____

Travel 1

```
L O T Z R M Y P N Q F S H S S S C C C
K Q E R U T R A P E D R W H Q M O G I
M P M K O O B E D I U G E N S B M H G
O G X L H S I J P I K I V B W N P R N
F N R J Y K B G A H L L D L L M A L J
Y P X O C C N N M E J O A S W C S M C
N Y F Q N B I I H H E M H I H M S B N
R E O U E I K K Q B T B V T L X Z A A
E N C J R P C O T W K O P F Q U N C N
Z R W L R S E O N P P R E V O M O K L
F U L N U U H B B O P D F O F I I P K
B O B S C N C V T N A E P V D S T A V
H J Z A B R O A D X U R A T C F A C M
S G B G T O S R A L U C O N I B N K J
R O I D K J U N N A D A P T E R I O U
B N Q S U R X X P V C R U I S E T Z H
Y T N X H C A M C O R D E R V M S J K
Y E M O U I Q T L A V I R R A Q E C I
S M O T S U C C A M E R A A O J D Z S
```

ABROAD	_____	ADAPTER	_____
ARRIVAL	_____	BACKPACK	_____
BINOCULARS	_____	BOOKING	_____
BORDER	_____	CAMCORDER	_____
CAMERA	_____	CHECK IN	_____
COMPASS	_____	CRUISE	_____
CURRENCY	_____	CUSTOMS	_____
DEPARTURE	_____	DESTINATION	_____
GUIDEBOOK	_____	HOLIDAY	_____
ID	_____	JOURNEY	_____

Solutions p. 75

Travel 2

```
V T E K C I T N R U T E R Z V J N M D
R P A K J V P O T A D R A C T S O P U
I D C C T Z T A G M P N D B T O P J J
M L Y V S L Z X S B T V F V G A S B U
V C Q Q I U E V H S N H T V S Q U H C
Q Q N T R G Q R J H E R G S L E I P G
U R K J U G X U U D I N P A N K T S A
G E K L O A G E T P F O G C Z X C O B
S T S H T G D N K R R I O E Z W A U G
E M O J L E K I I T O N R M R T S V N
S U T U O T K C Q E E S T A N C E E I
S R B R R E R Z Z W E I E Y F Z H N P
A A C Q Z V A Q A A C S W R G A Q I E
L W L G B X M Y K K D E T L J V S R E
G N O D S A D H E I X T B H X F S G L
N B K W B M N T E G F N Y N G T V V S
U Y J M G A A A B J J E M X K I G I Z
S H H J T B L C A C D T J W Y K S I Z
W T R A V E L A G E N C Y T X N Z P Z
```

LANDMARK	_____	LUGGAGE	_____
ONE-WAY	_____	PASSENGER	_____
PASSPORT	_____	POSTCARD	_____
RESORT	_____	RETURN TICKET	_____
SAFARI	_____	SIGHTSEEING	_____
SLEEPING BAG	_____	SOUVENIR	_____
SUITCASE	_____	SUNGLASSES	_____
TENT	_____	TICKET	_____
TOUR	_____	TOURIST	_____
TRAVEL AGENCY	_____	TRIP	_____

Places & Buildings 1

```
T  L  P  L  A  I  F  N  Z  L  B  A  K  E  R  Y  Y  C  Z
C  C  P  F  Z  T  V  V  H  A  H  B  X  A  N  S  H  D  F
Q  I  A  G  X  S  Q  H  C  F  L  A  S  Q  C  U  M  A  I
L  F  N  R  H  H  H  J  O  H  U  N  G  T  G  R  S  M  R
L  D  G  E  P  F  G  O  I  S  B  K  Y  S  E  Y  O  U  E
N  Z  V  O  M  A  D  E  G  Z  P  L  Y  H  A  U  M  S  S
N  E  E  F  E  A  R  O  D  C  B  I  C  A  L  H  F  E  T
T  S  C  O  U  R  T  K  K  T  H  T  T  N  P  B  U  M  A
B  O  O  K  S  T  O  R  E  R  U  U  O  A  N  U  Y  E  T
P  A  C  H  P  T  L  M  F  B  R  I  R  A  L  S  A  N  I
X  P  X  O  K  E  B  T  U  Q  T  P  Y  C  W  S  I  T  O
P  K  N  T  R  C  S  C  T  A  O  E  W  O  H  T  R  P  N
Q  Q  R  E  V  I  F  J  T  W  V  U  Q  N  W  O  P  A  T
H  J  D  L  R  N  F  S  E  I  T  I  O  W  E  P  O  R  L
N  R  E  O  V  V  S  D  F  U  Q  K  Y  P  M  Z  R  K  C
Y  X  L  X  E  A  Z  O  M  G  R  O  C  E  R  Y  T  S  A
W  F  N  F  G  N  G  S  X  Q  G  S  N  G  O  L  I  U  F
X  L  C  J  S  J  Y  I  O  F  A  C  T  O  R  Y  M  I  E
W  S  G  R  L  M  C  N  P  J  E  Q  Z  Q  T  M  Z  Y  V
```

AIRPORT	_____	AMUSEMENT PARK	_____
BAKERY	_____	BANK	_____
BOOKSTORE	_____	BUS STOP	_____
BUTCHER	_____	CAFÉ	_____
CAR PARK	_____	CHURCH	_____
CINEMA	_____	COURT	_____
FACTORY	_____	FIRE STATION	_____
FLORIST	_____	GAS STATION	_____
GROCERY	_____	GYM	_____
HOSPITAL	_____	HOTEL	_____

Places & Buildings 2

```
F T G G S S Y N A G O G U E W B Q P K
R P W J P L A Y G R O U N D R F G X P
E T W C E P L A U N D E R E T T E F O
S W S U P E R M A R K E T F I R P X L
T V J R B X C O P G V A X Q Y E O I I
A S Z P J S C O T O E T B R E H S Y C
U C S N R Z G S X H O O A K J B T Z E
R H U Y Y X V K T P A R L D W I O B S
A O T O W N H A L L B C F R S V F G T
N O P A R K I T W I R Q T R C R F X A
T L X T T L X I L D R I E E M R I G T
M O S Q U E A N P Y Y V O U M Q C D I
N H S K I E L G M H I V I J G P E Z O
C M T S X V U R N N A D K Z W U L Q N
R V A E Q D K I U T A R V E C M S E Z
N P T I P A Z N K T B M M S B W D W I
O E I G R S D K S B K P J A C R Y D X
T Q O Z E M Y M U S E U M Z C E W J S
A K N J B K M R Q H K E V H E Y F E K
```

LIBRARY _____
MOSQUE _____
PARK _____
PLAYGROUND _____
POST OFFICE _____
SCHOOL _____
STADIUM _____
SUPERMARKET _____
TEMPLE _____
TOWN HALL _____

LAUNDERETTE _____
MUSEUM _____
PHARMACY _____
POLICE STATION _____
RESTAURANT _____
SKATING RINK _____
STATION _____
SYNAGOGUE _____
THEATER _____
UNIVERSITY _____

Parts of the house 1

```
Z H X O D R I V E W A Y V J Y X C Q M
Y V B J B M E T A G K C Z F T N W G A
R K J A I B H G B O C T C E U Y R R C
U O F R S G A F N T D S Y N F P D E O
B W X T B E G L I I B X H C N S C E N
V S A A M B M A C E L A B E G Q E N S
R R G F O H G E R O L I T X C Y L H E
S O R Q O E Z Y N D N E E H E E L O R
O H O E R Z K J C T E Y L C R P A U V
M C U D G B S A P S G N N R F O R S A
Y P N P N W G T K C A U Z O E B O E T
M N D J I X X T O Q R L A D Y V I M O
F X F F N B H I L G A I Y I M L N F R
V S L O I E E C L K G E Z R M E I A Y
C T O M D S L D S E N K F R S F S R Z
X F O I N Z A N R M U B N O F C O T V
T C R O G X Z D I O T E E C U O T F V
W J Q G W K N H H B O Z K F L K L A Q
I D Q W R C C W R W H M W F Y D V O C
```

ATTIC   _____   BALCONY   _____

BASEMENT   _____   BATHROOM   _____

BEDROOM   _____   CEILING   _____

CELLAR   _____   CHIMNEY   _____

CONSERVATORY _____   CORRIDOR   _____

DINING ROOM   _____   DOOR   _____

DRIVEWAY   _____   FENCE   _____

FLOOR   _____   GARAGE   _____

GARDEN   _____   GATE   _____

GREENHOUSE   _____   GROUND FLOOR _____

Parts of the house 2

```
O S D S W I M M I N G P O O L R T J Y
Q Z V D W S D U D I K O R A U V Q D E
U Y D S I F F C B S N K E R D X N J M
C K O C N N M E R N Z U T I C C M S O
E A K G D E S I Y V D X T S L A Z H O
N D R O O F A O F W E G U S D U V U R
V S Q R W T K H W M H B G Y T S E T T
J R B Y S X T J G H S N H I N A Y T S
M B O S O E U O A J P A L O F C Z E E
O C J R L W I L Z F I I L F U V I R U
O X T I L T L P P O T F O A Z S F N G
R D O G A Z O A P Y G C U T X P E W F
G T W P Y M D P R K P X N C B J J T K
N T R D H B C O O S I F G T H T L K V
I S P T T F O C J R L T E Z E D U S D
V J B L A M P O G L C V C O U F K F A
I M Q W P Y Z I A Y F H M H A T X L R
L V C M H U Y W N O C L E B E P I N E
W F V L E T T E R B O X D D N N P W V
```

GUEST ROOM _____   GUTTER _____
HALL _____   HOUSE _____
KITCHEN _____   LETTERBOX _____
LIVING ROOM _____   LOUNGE _____
PATH _____   PATIO _____
PORCH _____   ROOF _____
SHED _____   SHUTTER _____
STAIRS _____   SWIMMING POOL _____
TOILET _____   UTILITY ROOM _____
WALL _____   WINDOW _____

Living room

```
W  N  H  L  E  E  S  X  I  G  Z  I  D  N  I  L  B  E  Y
D  X  I  B  T  G  Z  N  O  I  S  I  V  E  L  E  T  T  N
X  O  I  C  O  O  K  F  I  S  P  A  I  N  T  I  N  G  I
L  K  D  O  M  S  T  O  O  L  R  B  N  H  S  V  T  P  M
Q  I  S  F  E  R  R  E  P  N  F  G  A  R  K  O  I  F  X
M  N  B  F  R  E  P  G  E  R  U  T  I  N  R  U  F  Z  N
J  S  B  E  L  N  X  V  U  V  A  R  A  X  W  S  F  A  O
E  N  Z  E  T  O  F  H  E  X  M  R  G  O  L  V  V  N  I
I  I  I  T  V  I  X  Y  R  C  J  O  M  Y  V  J  R  L  H
E  A  R  A  X  T  U  T  O  U  B  J  K  C  Z  W  R  R  S
F  T  Q  B  X  I  X  I  T  K  I  E  X  C  H  U  P  Z  U
I  R  S  L  U  D  P  M  A  B  N  A  F  E  G  A  E  Q  C
R  U  H  E  B  N  Q  M  I  T  D  Q  M  O  T  T  I  H  W
E  C  E  F  H  O  P  E  D  M  M  S  T  E  Z  Y  A  R  I
P  L  L  J  J  C  N  L  A  A  X  F  P  B  D  W  R  V  S
L  L  V  M  Y  R  E  W  R  A  E  R  P  D  Z  O  T  N  L
A  E  E  M  H  I  F  Z  R  S  A  S  Q  P  V  R  E  C  H
C  G  S  A  W  A  A  A  M  C  E  S  A  V  H  V  A  H  W
E  J  F  O  O  T  R  E  S  T  B  F  Y  O  H  I  J  J  P
```

ARMCHAIR	_____	BLIND	_____
CARPET	_____	COFFEE TABLE	_____
CURTAINS	_____	CUSHION	_____
FAN	_____	FIREPLACE	_____
FOOTREST	_____	FURNITURE	_____
PAINTING	_____	AIR CONDITIONER	_____
RADIATOR	_____	REMOTE	_____
RUG	_____	SHELVES	_____
SOFA	_____	STOOL	_____
TELEVISION	_____	VASE	_____

Bedroom

```
W  P  Z  Q  C  Y  Z  R  O  H  E  A  D  B  O  A  R  D  A
A  I  Y  C  H  E  S  T  O  F  D  R  A  W  E  R  S  A  L
F  L  P  D  L  L  N  S  F  K  R  D  O  B  E  R  V  L  T
J  L  R  P  R  L  B  Q  T  M  E  L  D  G  G  X  J  A  X
N  O  T  J  U  B  Q  E  W  B  L  E  N  F  X  X  P  R  Z
P  W  S  P  Q  M  K  R  E  I  B  A  S  K  D  Q  B  M  C
H  C  Z  D  M  N  O  L  P  E  H  M  E  J  U  K  E  C  Y
T  A  S  S  A  G  G  K  L  I  K  B  L  J  V  W  D  L  V
R  S  Q  L  Z  N  Y  B  K  C  O  X  A  E  E  Z  S  O  F
V  E  B  F  I  K  U  E  B  R  T  F  M  N  T  S  I  C  K
L  I  B  S  Y  O  F  D  D  T  L  W  P  H  E  W  D  K  L
E  G  U  O  D  H  L  R  V  S  R  K  H  R  N  B  E  S  L
O  P  N  S  R  S  A  W  B  A  Z  L  T  F  G  E  T  K  C
D  R  K  N  S  W  L  X  A  W  A  T  O  H  B  D  A  L  I
D  L  B  O  H  G  U  Y  M  R  A  A  T  R  B  B  B  N  G
X  J  E  M  E  S  V  Z  O  M  H  J  T  Y  F  A  L  G  O
D  F  D  M  E  R  Y  S  O  F  A  B  E  D  M  S  E  X  C
D  H  S  S  T  W  G  I  T  F  A  N  B  Q  M  E  P  K  X
H  R  B  E  D  S  I  D  E  L  A  M  P  Z  O  N  R  K  T
```

ALARM CLOCK	_____	BED	_____
BED BASE	_____	BEDSIDE LAMP	_____
BEDSIDE TABLE	_____	BLANKET	_____
BUNK BEDS	_____	CHEST OF DRAWERS	_____
DOUBLE BED	_____	DUVET	_____
HANGER	_____	HEADBOARD	_____
LAMP	_____	MATTRESS	_____
PILLOW	_____	PILLOWCASE	_____
SHEET	_____	SINGLE BED	_____
SOFA BED	_____	WARDROBE	_____

Kitchen 1

```
J K N R E H S A W H S I D H H W H J C
P Z D E X I J W Y R L Z I H E G C M C
N P B K Y F S Q N M R T K L A C Q P C
I B G Y L F Y E V G Z M T G C U K K L
K C O O K E R H O O D T J O O P G N N
I R C R W J D K Z J E Y J N O T E A C
J E U T P J Y E V K N X R R K B J P R
K K P L O J U R B N L D E L E J F G U
H A B W Y O E O O X H P W U R L I N Q
G M O M S A W R C Q A Q E F Y V Z I K
R E A U A L P X E P D G P Q D T B Y W
A E R P A A F E N D D J O M F F O R K
T F D P H R P E L I N O V F G O Z F H
E F V Y E J H V R K M A Z W W Z M O V
R O V E S C J F M U Z B L M W L B Y I
M C Z N T K P P N C U F Y O C I X A K
Q E Q I J N Z G L A S S U I C F Q K Y
R F K G F B L E N D E R P V A H H X A
Y N C H O P P I N G B O A R D O S S D
```

APRON	_____	BLENDER	_____
BOWL	_____	CHOPPING BOARD	_____
COFFEE MAKER	_____	COLANDER	_____
COOKER	_____	COOKER HOOD	_____
CUP	_____	CUPBOARD	_____
DISHWASHER	_____	FORK	_____
FREEZER	_____	FRIDGE	_____
FRYING PAN	_____	GLASS	_____
GRATER	_____	HOB	_____
KETTLE	_____	KITCHEN PAPER	_____

Kitchen 2

```
V X S A L A D B O W L X J M X D P D I
S J S A U C E P A N P P L P O E X G Y
L T M I C R O W A V E Z Q L V Z J H G
P M V S U P Y K M I X S H O N A P E T
R O Y T E A P O T K C K L O X W F T Z
E V B P U T S P O O N G O Q R F N E E
S T E A T O W E L E N P N K E C F A Y
S R M Y J L A D L E S I N K X K Y S P
U T P J O U U R V E P P L A T E G P E
R J A X T W S O L N X L F G Q L W O V
E B X S T R J B I D T B Q H N H Y O J
C Y K L U V A L U T O R U C V R H N H
O W U N X T L E V J A H C I X W L I E
O P O S I O V Y E Q S X W O R K T O P
K S U C R F R L U T T J X U D L F X I
E M I A A H E O F T E A Y X T K Q F G
R S J L F Q O V E N R K W Y U W K K T
V K D E T W Q Y F Z G G N A P K I N I
Z B I B W J M N B K M K M H A Z L D I
```

KNIFE	_____	LADLE	_____
MICROWAVE	_____	NAPKIN	_____
OVEN	_____	OVEN GLOVE	_____
PLATE	_____	PRESSURE COOKER	_____
ROLLIN PIN	_____	SALAD BOWL	_____
SAUCEPAN	_____	SCALE	_____
SINK	_____	SPOON	_____
TABLESPOON	_____	TEA TOWEL	_____
TEAPOT	_____	TEASPOON	_____
TOASTER	_____	WORKTOP	_____

Bathroom

```
O Q K U L H S U R B H T O O T P R X G
T O F E F K R D M X R T N V D H L X D
U B W Z E J W O S K V O Z F R X S C M
N O R F N Q C F A P A O S L C W V B W
T T O B L F O H E I B T B R U S H K C
L A Z P O W N I S A B H S A W X O D S
A D A D A D B Q L Q H P T C R D N M H
B N R W J T U J Y W J A J Y Z S B V E
B G S Z S H I B M J Q S P V H U A L B
A A P K X N P X N E L T I O S O T P O
T I M B O P B U Q O Y E W A J M H C R
H O O P M A H S E L T E X U X Q T S H
M A P N C F M B T K R T A I Y G U R T
A K B A D R W E E Y A M O H K N B Z A
T Y C E O G C K F O W M Q C L T N H B
R O M R T U K G R E Y R D R I A H G Y
E X R I A H T X I Y G F J A E U P O L
Z I I F T J B O Q D G C G R N G U M R
M R U A Q S H O W E R C U R T A I N K
```

BATH MAT	_____	BATHROBE	_____
BATHTUB	_____	BRUSH	_____
COMB	_____	COTTON BUD	_____
FAUCET	_____	HAIR DRYER	_____
MAKE-UP	_____	MIRROR	_____
RAZOR	_____	SHAMPOO	_____
SHOWER	_____	SHOWER CURTAIN	_____
SOAP	_____	TAP	_____
TOOTHBRUSH	_____	TOOTHPASTE	_____
TOWEL	_____	WASHBASIN	_____

Solutions p. 78

Utility room

```
D W W A S H I N G M A C H I N E N E R
F R E C Y C L I N G B I N Z I B G S R
A H W E P O M H Y X O R V P B K K R E
L C O D Z V F N C A Q O N Y U B O O Y
R A L T W S O H T C Q O Q Z C V W H R
E E M E I R L E J I O G T M K P C S D
K L R K I T Y B V W B H O R E U W E E
A B E S I P S O W F U O B D T D P H L
E C D A D H U I Y B R H X V R M L T B
R L D B U L R L Q B S O N A U G T O M
B O A Y S R T E O G B X O U D P I L U
T T L R T O F R M L E B C J H D H C T
I H P D P S S D O I G A P B Y M O H A
U E E N A H H O N N V M F G Z L A B N
C S T U N W T F I L K V N Z S W P F R
R P S A A J K N U W V D C L G U U M D
I I T L T X O U D E T E R G E N T S M
C N T L P R N N A V P L U N G E R H P
H O U T I Q M J B H I V W H U G U O W
```

BLEACH	_____	BOILER	_____
BROOM	_____	BUCKET	_____
CIRCUIT BREAKER	_____	CLOTHESHORSE	_____
CLOTHESPIN	_____	DETERGENT	_____
DUSTPAN	_____	IRON	_____
IRONING BOARD	_____	LAUNDRY BASKET	_____
MOP	_____	PLUNGER	_____
RECYCLING BIN	_____	STEPLADDER	_____
TOOLBOX	_____	TUMBLE DRYER	_____
VACUUM	_____	WASHING MACHINE	_____

On the road

```
V U F A Y T R A F F I C L I G H T S D
O K H F V P A V E M E N T B T Z N C M
S N X I S J M O J W L L C W O M W H F
R E K R F T X C L Y T A P V L S T N H
O M G E U S R P V A K S M Y L A L J S
U T K H U T N E I U D Z A P P N Q V P
N R L Y Z U H U E F Z W O E P F G A E
D A Y D X N I H T T H G L L K O M O D
A F K R L N C M V G D C A I P G S T E
B F G A Y E N Y I Y Y R R Q D M E T S
O I Z N S L V H Y C V T Q E R U X F T
U C Y T O K I P Y Q U H R N U X I U R
T J O P C R O S S W A L K M J I T B I
W A M G Y W F G I H P R W W A S J I A
B M B R I D G E U N D E R P A S S N
Z V H Q K L N R N P L O P V C I T C F
I M X N S H O U L D E R G U P U M D X
Y O T S D M A N H O L E R R J N Q O U
M X Y W C U O N E W A Y S T R E E T G
```

BRIDGE	_____	CROSSWALK	_____
CYCLE PATH	_____	EXIT	_____
FIRE HYDRANT	_____	HIGHWAY	_____
LAMPPOST	_____	MANHOLE	_____
ONE-WAY STREET	_____	PAVEMENT	_____
PEDESTRIAN	_____	ROUNDABOUT	_____
SHOULDER	_____	SIGN	_____
STREET	_____	TOLL	_____
TRAFFIC JAM	_____	TRAFFIC LIGHTS	_____
TUNNEL	_____	UNDERPASS	_____

Solutions p. 78

Means of transport

```
E O R U Q P I S H K L E O O D U J R N
J O E N G C N V G B L S U B W A Y M T
Z M N D H W S E H T T F C X T I Y O U
H T I E O S K H E L C Y C R O T O M T
M E R R L I P B T K A S Q V Y S T R E
H K A G B T D N W N V U S U S P U G H
J C M R O E M O P E D M S H Z C Z P S
U O B O M N A V A R A C I K K B T S X
Y R U U P K W O D S W P K A G W E I X
K Z S N R J R E T P O C I L E H O O D
W V B D T K T C J Q R O F T Y T G R T
E U S C H G A S L L O R R Y H K A R Q
C Y T P E R B T C C M A W R N O K Q B
S T E W B N I O F O I L V G B Y O M B
W B B O A T A N S N O K M E Q U I G N
F M L T S G L L O B V T T S T C X W P
X V W S B B M T P E E A E I Y K S G F
S O Z G Q D L F N Q K V N R D U G U O
D V O F K W K Q W S Q V Y B B C R P G
```

BIKE	_____	BOAT	_____
BUS	_____	CAR	_____
CARAVAN	_____	HELICOPTER	_____
LORRY	_____	MOPED	_____
MOTORCYCLE	_____	PLANE	_____
ROCKET	_____	SCOOTER	_____
SHIP	_____	SKATEBOARD	_____
SUBMARINE	_____	SUBWAY	_____
TRAIN	_____	TRUCK	_____
UNDERGROUND	_____	VAN	_____

Car parts

```
F  S  G  L  O  V  E  C  O  M  P  A  R  T  M  E  N  T  Z
K  Q  N  S  S  T  E  E  R  I  N  G  W  H  E  E  L  X  P
H  A  N  D  B  R  A  K  E  G  Y  J  B  W  J  B  D  O  G
X  A  N  K  P  M  G  H  S  U  J  G  C  N  K  L  J  R  R
J  D  Z  Z  C  M  E  T  P  L  D  Y  G  J  E  D  Z  E  K
F  P  H  D  L  G  A  W  S  O  X  D  U  I  Q  U  R  A  N
F  D  K  X  U  G  R  H  P  E  I  B  H  N  E  E  G  R  V
E  V  T  Z  T  O  L  E  R  X  A  S  G  T  P  D  B  V  Q
X  L  O  M  C  T  E  E  O  W  D  T  A  I  L  A  P  I  N
H  B  D  G  H  Y  V  L  U  N  P  L  W  U  H  S  E  E  H
A  S  M  I  B  S  E  O  I  X  P  A  S  B  J  H  F  W  J
U  F  D  J  F  Z  R  W  S  E  T  E  C  P  Y  B  K  M  D
S  B  U  M  P  E  R  S  B  N  Z  V  H  Q  O  F  I  M
T  E  K  J  C  E  J  N  V  I  T  S  J  X  S  A  D  R  M
P  F  J  D  X  F  E  P  G  X  I  Z  Q  K  F  R  W  R  O
I  E  U  E  W  C  N  N  F  Q  R  T  K  E  D  D  B  O  Y
P  T  Y  N  I  E  E  H  D  T  E  F  H  O  R  N  D  R  Q
E  E  K  L  N  A  J  S  E  A  T  B  E  L  T  P  W  I  G
B  J  I  N  D  I  C  A  T  O  R  B  A  T  T  E  R  Y  S
```

BATTERY	_____	BUMPER	_____
CLUTCH	_____	DASHBOARD	_____
ENGINE	_____	EXHAUST PIPE	_____
GEAR LEVER	_____	GLOVE COMPARTMENT	_____
HANDBRAKE	_____	HORN	_____
INDICATOR	_____	LICENSE PLATE	_____
REARVIEW MIRROR	_____	SEAT	_____
SEAT BELT	_____	STEERING WHEEL	_____
TIRE	_____	WHEEL	_____
WINDSHIELD	_____	WIPER	_____

Solutions p. 79

Tools

```
A  L  A  D  I  P  S  C  R  E  W  D  R  I  V  E  R  F  O
L  Y  J  D  R  S  I  C  S  D  F  A  H  Q  Z  L  M  W  E
U  K  N  F  S  D  R  C  M  M  K  B  A  R  V  I  Z  Q  F
H  B  P  Z  Y  R  Z  A  K  U  B  D  E  S  P  C  P  Z  W
C  O  L  J  N  S  O  E  E  A  K  J  E  W  T  E  H  V  J
N  T  I  W  M  T  Z  M  R  H  X  R  D  K  V  B  O  J  Y
E  X  E  L  C  P  Q  A  E  J  S  E  R  W  E  N  K  P  L
R  I  R  J  S  S  O  L  M  H  P  Y  V  E  M  X  Z  F  E
W  L  S  B  Z  E  E  L  M  C  A  D  J  C  D  U  X  Q  V
E  F  R  U  B  B  P  E  A  R  U  S  J  U  F  D  A  X  E
L  E  O  P  N  Q  G  T  H  O  Y  N  J  D  Q  H  A  S  L
B  X  G  Q  D  T  A  D  D  T  V  A  F  E  K  A  R  L  T
A  A  Q  H  O  S  E  V  R  U  H  Z  H  W  S  L  W  O  I
T  N  P  C  U  T  T  E  R  I  A  C  A  D  C  R  L  Q  R
S  W  U  S  D  S  Z  A  M  C  L  S  D  F  V  R  E  K  I
U  S  Q  V  N  J  O  G  N  T  P  L  T  L  Z  K  V  T  P
J  H  J  F  R  E  W  O  M  N  W  A  L  Z  U  Y  O  N  S
D  T  T  P  D  E  R  U  S  A  E  M  E  P  A  T  H  G  Y
A  L  H  L  W  H  E  E  L  B  A  R  R  O  W  U  S  B  F
```

ADJUSTABLE WRENCH_____	AXE	_____
CUTTER _____	DRILL	_____
HAMMER _____	HOSE	_____
LADDER _____	LAWN MOWER	_____
MALLET _____	PICKAXE	_____
PLIERS _____	RAKE	_____
SAW _____	SCREWDRIVER	_____
SHEARS _____	SHOVEL	_____
SPIRIT LEVEL _____	TAPE MEASURE	_____
TORCH _____	WHEELBARROW	_____

Merci d'avoir choisi notre livre !

Votre avis est important pour notre équipe, nous apprécierions grandement si vous pouviez le partager sur Amazon.

Pour ce faire, rendez-vous
sur la page Amazon de ce livre et
cliquez sur "Ecrire un commentaire client".

NOTE

Pour optimiser votre apprentissage et mémoriser par la répétition le vocabulaire appris, nous vous proposons de combiner cette édition avec le livre de mots croisés débutant de notre collection.

Ce dernier reprend le même lexique dans une version innovante pour vous permettre de faire une révision.

Le principe est de trouver la traduction à l'aide des lettres mélangées du vocabulaire que vous avez vu dans les mots mêlés.

Voici la grille du thème SHOPPING que vous pourrez faire après avoir fini celle des mots mêlés.

Pour retrouver le livre des mots croisés ainsi que notre collection, scannez le QR code qui se trouve au dos du livre.

SHOPPING À TESTER

Across / Horizontal
1. Chariot / LYRELOT
3. Caissier / EHAIRSC
7. Remboursement / UDERFN
9. Portefeuille / TLWLAE
12. Solde / LESA
13. Cabine d'essayage / GFTITIN OMRO
14. Caisse / HCCEK TUO
15. Caisse enregistreuse / ILTL
16. Bonne affaire / NGIRBAA
17. Bon marché / HECAP

Down / Vertical
2. Reçu / CEEPTRI
4. Vendeur / OSPH AINTSASST
5. Rayon / LEHFS
6. Client / REOMTUSC
8. Panier / EKATSB
10. Cher / EPNXEESIV
11. Queue / UUEEQ
16. Sac / AGB
17. Espèces / ASHC
18. Porte-monnaie / SUPRE

53

Scanner le QR Code pour écouter la prononciation des mots qui se trouvent dans le lexique.

Le **Password** est : **izycode**

Vous pouvez aussi y accéder en recopiant l'URL **izylingo.com/audio.vd** dans la barre d'adresse de votre navigateur.

N'hésitez pas à nous contacter en cas de besoin à l'adresse mail suivante: contact@izylingo.com

Lexique

Page 2 **Days & Months**

Monday	Lundi	April	Avril
Tuesday	Mardi	May	Mai
Wednesday	Mercredi	June	Juin
Thursday	Jeudi	July	Juillet
Friday	Vendredi	August	Août
Saturday	Samedi	September	Septembre
Sunday	Dimanche	October	Octobre
January	Janvier	November	Novembre
February	Février	December	Décembre
March	Mars	Weekend	Week-end

Page 3 **Weather**

Autumn	Automne	Rain	Pluie
Cloudy	Nuageux	Rainbow	Arc-en-ciel
Cold	Froid	Snow	Neige
Drought	Sécheresse	Spring	Printemps
Dry	Sec	Storm	Tempête
Fog	Brouillard	Summer	Eté
Heat wave	Canicule	Sunny	Ensoleillé
Hot	Chaud	Wet	Humide
Mist	Brume	Windy	Venteux
Overcast	Couvert	Winter	Hiver

Page 4 **Numbers**

One	Un	Eleven	Onze
Two	Deux	Twelve	Douze
Three	Trois	Thirteen	Treize
Four	Quatre	Fourteen	Quatorze
Five	Cinq	Fifteen	Quinze
Six	Six	Sixteen	Seize
Seven	Sept	Seventeen	Dix-sept
Eight	Huit	Eighteen	Dix-huit
Nine	Neuf	Nineteen	Dix-neuf
Ten	Dix	Twenty	Vingt

Page 5 **Colors**

Beige	Beige	Multicolored	Multicolore
Black	Noir	Navy	Bleu marine
Blue	Bleu	Orange	Orange
Bronze	Bronze	Pink	Rose
Brown	Marron	Purple	Violet
Dark	Foncé	Red	Rouge
Gold	Or	Silver	Argent
Green	Vert	Turquoise	Turquoise
Grey	Gris	White	Blanc
Light	Clair	Yellow	Jaune

Lexique

Page 6 **Common Verbs 1**

Ask	Demander	Give	Donner
Buy	Acheter	Go	Aller
Close	Fermer	Help	Aider
Come	Venir	Know	Savoir
Cook	Cuisiner	Learn	Apprendre
Drink	Boire	Leave	Partir
Drive	Conduire	Like	Aimer
Eat	Manger	Look	Regarder
Find	Trouver	Make	Faire
Follow	Suivre	Open	Ouvrir

Page 7 **Common Verbs 2**

Pay	Payer	Take	Prendre
Play	Jouer	Tell	Raconter
Put	Mettre	Try	Essayer
Read	Lire	Understand	Comprendre
Run	Courir	Use	Utiliser
Say	Dire	Wait	Attendre
See	Voir	Walk	Marcher
Sleep	Dormir	Want	Vouloir
Speak	Parler	Work	Travailler
Start	Commencer	Write	Écrire

Page 8 **Preposition of place**

Above	Au-dessus de	In front of	Devant
Around	Autour de	Inside	À l'intérieur de
At	À	Near	Proche de
Behind	Derrière	Next to	À côté de
Below	En dessous	On	Sur
Beside	Auprès de	Opposite	À l'opposé de
Between	Entre	Outside	À l'extérieur de
Close to	Près de	Over	Par-dessus
Far from	Loin de	Under	Sous
In	Dans	Underneath	Au-dessous de

Page 9 **Family**

Aunt	Tante	Mother	Mère
Brother	Frère	Nephew	Neveu
Cousin	Cousin/cousine	Niece	Nièce
Daughter	Fille	Parents	Parents
Father	Père	Parents-in-law	Beaux-parents
Granddaughter	Petite-fille	Sister	Sœur
Grandfather	Grand-père	Son	Fils
Grandmother	Grand-mère	Spouse	Époux/Épouse
Grandson	Petit-fils	Uncle	Oncle
Husband	Mari	Wife	Femme/Epouse

Lexique

Page 10 The head

Beard	Barbe	Hair	Cheveux
Cheek	Joue	Head	Tête
Chin	Menton	Lips	Lèvres
Ear	Oreille	Moustache	Moustache
Eye	Œil	Mouth	Bouche
Eyebrow	Sourcil	Nose	Nez
Eyelashes	Cils	Nostril	Narine
Eyelid	Paupière	Temple	Tempe
Face	Visage	Tongue	Langue
Forehead	Front	Tooth	Dent

Page 11 The body

Ankle	Cheville	Knee	Genou
Arm	Bras	Leg	Jambe
Back	Dos	Neck	Cou
Calf	Molet	Shin	Tibia
Chest	Poitrine	Shoulder	Épaule
Elbow	Coude	Stomach	Ventre
Finger	Doigt	Thigh	Cuisse
Foot	Pied	Toe	Orteil
Hand	Main	Waist	Taille
Heel	Talon	Wrist	Poignet

Page 12 Physical Appearance

Bald	Chauve	Short	Court
Bearded	Barbu	Slim	Mince
Beautiful	Beau	Small	Petit
Big	Gros/Grand	Strong	Fort
Fat	Gros	Tall	Grand
Hairy	Poilu	Thin	Maigre
Long	Long	Ugly	Laid
Medium	Moyen	Muscular	Musclé
Old	Vieux	Wrinkled	Ridé
Pretty	Joli	Young	Jeune

Page 13 Characters

Active	Actif	Lazy	Paresseux
Bossy	Autoritaire	Nasty	Méchant
Brave	Courageux	Nice	Gentil
Clever	Intelligent	Patient	Patient
Curious	Curieux	Polite	Poli
Dishonest	Malhonnête	Selfish	Egoïste
Fair	Juste	Sensitive	Sensible
Funny	Drôle	Shy	Timide
Generous	Généreux	Silly	Stupide
Honest	Honnête	Stubborn	Têtu

Lexique

Page 14 **Feelings 1**

Afraid	Peur	Embarrassed	Gêné
Amazed	Étonné	Excited	Excité
Angry	En colère	Exhausted	Épuisé
Bored	Ennuyé	Frightened	Effrayé
Calm	Calme	Furious	Furieux
Cautious	Prudent	Glad	Content
Confident	Confiant	Happy	Heureux
Depressed	Déprimé	Hopeless	Désespéré
Disappointed	Déçu	Impressed	Impressionné
Disgusted	Dégoûté	Interested	Intéressé

Page 15 **Feelings 2**

Jealous	Jaloux	Shocked	Choqué
Joyful	Joyeux	Sick	Malade
Nervous	Nerveux	Stressed	Stressé
Pensive	Pensif	Surprised	Surpris
Pleased	Content	Tired	Fatigué
Proud	Fier	Unhappy	Malheureux
Relaxed	Détendu	Upset	Contrarié
Sad	Triste	Weak	Faible
Satisfied	Satisfait	Well	Bien
Scared	Effrayé	Worried	Inquiet

Page 16 **Restaurant**

Bill	Facture	Order	Commander
Chips	Frites (GB)	Pepper	Poivre
Delivery	Livraison	Rare	Saignant
Dessert	Dessert	Salt	Sel
Drink	Boisson	Sauce	Sauce
Fries	Frites (USA)	Spicy	Épicé
Grill	Grillade	Straw	Paille
Meal	Repas	Take away	Emporter
Medium rare	À point	Tip	Pourboire
Menu	Menu/Carte	Well-done	Bien cuit

Page 17 **Food**

Biscuit	Biscuit	Jam	Confiture
Bread	Pain	Meat	Viande
Butter	Beurre	Milk	Lait
Cake	Gâteau	Pasta	Pâtes
Cereal	Céréale	Rice	Riz
Cheese	Fromage	Sandwich	Sandwich
Egg	Oeuf	Sausage	Saucisse
Fish	Poisson	Seafood	Fruit de mer
Ham	Jambon	Tuna	Thon
Ice cream	Glace	Yogurt	Yaourt

Lexique

Page 18 **Fruits 1**

Apple	Pomme	Date	Date
Apricot	Abricot	Dried fruit	Fruit sec
Avocado	Avocat	Fig	Figue
Banana	Banane	Fresh fruit	Fruit frais
Blackberry	Mûre	Fruit juice	Jus de fruit
Blueberry	Myrtille	Fruit salad	Salade de fruits
Cherry	Cerise	Fruit tree	Arbre fruitier
Citrus	Agrume	Grape	Raisins
Clementine	Clémentine	Grapefruit	Pamplemousse
Coconut	Noix de coco	Kiwi	Kiwi

Page 19 **Fruits 2**

Lemon	Citron	Peach	Pêche
Lime	Citron vert	Pear	Poire
Lychee	Litchi	Persimmon	Kaki
Mandarin	Mandarine	Pineapple	Ananas
Mango	Mangue	Pip	Pépin
Melon	Melon	Plum	Prune
Nectarine	Nectarine	Pomegranate	Grenade
Orange	Orange	Raspberry	Framboise
Papaya	Papaye	Strawberry	Fraise
Passion fruit	Fruit de la passion	Watermelon	Pastèque

Page 20 **Vegetables 1**

Artichoke	Artichaut	Cherry tomato	Tomate cerise
Asparagus	Asperge	Chilli	Piment
Bean	Haricot	Chives	Ciboulette
Beetroot	Betterave	Corn	Maïs
Broccoli	Brocoli	Courgette	Courgette
Brussels sprout	Choux de Bruxelles	Cucumber	Concombre
Cabbage	Choux	Eggplant	Aubergine
Carrot	Carotte	Endive	Endive
Cauliflower	Choux fleur	Garlic	Ail
Celery	Céleri	Gherkin	Cornichon

Page 21 **Vegetables 2**

Ginger	Gingembre	Pumpkin	Citrouille
Leek	Poireau	Radish	Radis
Lentils	Lentilles	Rhubarb	Rhubarbe
Lettuce	Laitue	Shallot	Échalote
Mushroom	Champignon	Soya	Soja
Onion	Oignon	Spinach	Épinards
Organic	Bio	Squash	Courge
Pea	Petit pois	Sweet potato	Patate douce
Pepper	Poivron	Tomato	Tomate
Potato	Pomme de terre	Turnip	Navet

Lexique

Page 22 Pets & Farm animals

Cat	Chat	Hamster	Hamster
Chicken	Poule	Horse	Cheval
Cock	Coq	Mouse	Souris
Cow	Vache	Parrot	Perroquet
Dog	Chien	Pig	Cochon
Donkey	Âne	Pony	Poney
Duck	Canard	Rabbit	Lapin
Frog	Grenouille	Sheep	Mouton
Goat	Chèvre	Turkey	Dinde
Goldfish	Poisson rouge	Turtle	Tortue

Page 23 Wild animals

Bat	Chauve-souris	Koala	Koala
Bear	Ours	Lion	Lion
Camel	Chameau	Monkey	Singe
Crocodile	Crocodile	Owl	Hibou
Elephant	Éléphant	Panda	Panda
Fox	Renard	Rhinoceros	Rhinocéros
Giraffe	Girafe	Snake	Serpent
Gorilla	Gorille	Tiger	Tigre
Hippopotamus	Hippopotame	Wolf	Loup
Kangaroo	Kangourou	Zebra	Zèbre

Pages 24 Insects

Ant	Fourmi	Fly	Mouche
Bee	Abeille	Grasshopper	Sauterelle
Beetle	Scarabée	Hornet	Frelon
Butterfly	Papillon	Ladybird	Coccinelle
Caterpillar	Chenille	Lice	Poux
Cicada	Cigale	Mosquito	Moustique
Cockroach	Cafard	Spider	Araignée
Cricket	Criquet	Termite	Termite
Dragonfly	Libellule	Wasp	Guêpe
Flea	Puce	Worm	Ver

Page 25 Hobbies

Biking	Cyclisme	Hunting	Chasse
Camping	Camping	Painting	Peinture
Cooking	Cuisine	Photography	Photographie
Diving	Plongée	Pottery	Poterie
DIY	Bricolage	Reading	Lecture
Drawing	Dessin	Riding	Équitation
Fishing	Pêche	Sailing	Voile
Gaming	Jeux	Sewing	Couture
Gardening	Jardinage	Traveling	Voyager
Hiking	Randonnée	Walk	Promenade

Lexique

Page 26 Jobs 1

Accountant	Comptable	Electrician	Électricien
Actor	Acteur	Engineer	Ingénieur
Architect	Architecte	Farmer	Agriculteur
Astronaut	Astronaute	Firefighter	Sapeur-pompier
Baker	Boulanger	Fisherman	Pêcheur
Bricklayer	Maçon	Gardener	Jardinier
Cook	Cuisinier	Grocer	Épicier
Dentist	Dentist	Hairdresser	Coiffeur
Doctor	Docteur	Jeweller	Bijoutier
Driver	Chauffeur	Journalist	Journaliste

Page 27 Jobs 2

judge	Juge	Plumber	Plombier
Lawyer	Avocat	Police officer	Policier
Manager	Directeur	Postman	Facteur
Mechanic	Mécanicien	Secretary	Secrétaire
Musician	Musicien	Seller	Vendeur
Nurse	Infirmière	Singer	Chanteur
Painter	Peintre	Stewardess	Hôtesse de l'air
Pharmacist	Pharmacien	Vet	Vétérinaire
Photographer	Photographe	Waiter	Serveur
Pilot	Pilote	Writer	Écrivain

Page 28 The classroom 1

Bin	Corbeille	Colored pencils	Crayons de couleur
Blackboard	Tableau	Desk	Bureau
Book	Livre	Eraser	Effaceur
Bookcase	Bibliothèque	File	Dossier
Calculator	Calculatrice	Glue	Colle
Chair	Chaise	Highlighter	Surligneur
Chalk	Craie	Map	Carte
Clock	Horloge	Marker	Marqueur
Compass	Compas	Notebook	Cahier
Computer	Ordinateur	Paint	Peinture

Page 29 The classroom 2

Paintbrush	Pinceau	Ruler	Règle
paper clip	trombone	Schoolbag	Cartable
Pen	Stylo	Scissors	Ciseaux
Pencil	Crayon à papier	Sheet	Feuille
Pencil case	Trousse	Slate	Ardoise
Pencil sharpener	Taille-crayon	Stapler	Agrafeuse
Pin	Épingle	Student	Étudiant/Élève
Projector	Vidéoprojecteur	Table	Table
Protractor	Rapporteur	Tape	Ruban adhésif
Rubber	Gomme	Teacher	Enseignant

Lexique

Page 30 Exam

Answer	Réponse	Instructions	Instructions
Cheat	Tricher	Match	Apparier
Difficult	Difficile	Memorize	Mémoriser
Easy	Facile	Mistake	Erreur
Essay	Dissertation	Multiple choice	Choix multiple
Examiner	Examinateur	Pass	Réussir
Fail	Échouer	Question	Question
False	FAUX	Revise	Réviser
Grade	Note	True	VRAI
Guess	Deviner	Wrong	Mauvais

Page 31 Shopping

Bag	Sac	Purse	Porte-monnaie
Bargain	Bonne affaire	Queue	Queue
Basket	Panier	Receipt	Reçu
Cash	Espèces	Refund	Remboursement
Cashier	Caissier	Sale	Solde
Cheap	Bon marché	Shelf	Rayon
Check out	Caisse	Shop assistant	Vendeur
Customer	Client	Till	Caisse enregistreuse
Expensive	Cher	Trolley	Chariot
Fitting room	Cabine d'essayage	Wallet	Portefeuille

Page 32 Clothes 1

Belt	Ceinture	Jacket	Veste
Boots	Bottes	Jeans	Jean
Bra	Soutien-gorge	Jumper	Pull (2)
Cap	Casquette/Bonnet	Knickers	Culotte
Cardigan	Cardigan	Pants	Pantalon (USA)
Coat	Manteau	Pyjamas	Pyjama
Dress	Robe	Raincoat	Imperméable
Flip-flops	Tongs	Sandal	Sandale
Gloves	Gants	Scarf	Écharpe/Foulard
Hat	Chapeau	Shirt	Chemise

Page 33 Clothes 2

Shoes	Chaussures	T-shirt	Tee-shirt
Shorts	Short	Tank top	Débardeur
Skirt	Jupe	Tie	Cravate
Slippers	Pantoufles	Tights	Collants
Sneakers	Baskets (USA)	Tracksuit	Survêtement
Socks	Chaussettes	Trainers	Baskets (GB)
Stockings	Bas	Trousers	Pantalon (GB)
Suit	Costume	Underwear	Sous-vêtements
Sweater	Pull (1)	Uniform	Uniforme
Swimsuit	Maillot de bain	Vest	Gilet

Lexique

Page 34 **Nature**

Air	Air	Plant	Plante
Cloud	Nuage	Sand	Sable
Earth	Terre	Sky	Ciel
Fire	Feu	Stars	Étoiles
Flower	Fleur	Stone	Pierre
Grass	Herbe	Sun	Soleil
Human being	Être humain	Tree	Arbre
Ice	Glace	Water	Eau
Leaf	Feuille	Wind	Vent
Moon	Lune	Wood	Bois

Page 35 **Landscape**

Cave	Grotte	Jungle	Jungle
City	Ville	Lake	Lac
Cliff	Falaise	Mountain	Montagne
Countryside	Campagne	Ocean	Océan
Desert	Désert	Pond	Étang
Field	Champ	River	Rivière
Flood	Inondation	Sea	Mer
Forest	Forêt	Valley	Vallée
Hill	Colline	Volcano	Volcan
Island	Île	Waterfall	Cascade

Page 36 **Travel 1**

Abroad	À l'étranger	Compass	Boussole
Adapter	Adaptateur	Cruise	Croisière
Arrival	Arrivée	Currency	Devise
Backpack	Sac à dos	Customs	Douane
Binoculars	Jumelles	Departure	Départ
Booking	Réservation	Destination	Destination
Border	Frontière	Guidebook	Guide de voyage
Camcorder	Caméscope	Holiday	Vacances
Camera	Appareil photo	ID	Pièce d'identité
Check in	S'enregistrer	Journey	Trajet

Page 37 **Travel 2**

Landmark	Monument	Sleeping bag	Sac de couchage
Luggage	Bagage	Souvenir	Souvenir
One-way	Aller simple	Suitcase	Valise
Passenger	Passager	Sunglasses	Lunettes de soleil
Passport	Passeport	Tent	Tentes
Postcard	Carte postal	Ticket	Billet
Resort	Station de vacances	Tour	Tour de visite
Return ticket	Aller-retour	Tourist	Touriste
Safari	Safari	Travel agency	Agence de voyages
Sightseeing	Visite touristique	Trip	Excursion

Lexique

Page 38 **Places & Buildings 1**

Airport	Aéroport	Cinema	Cinéma
Amusement park	Parc d'attractions	Court	Tribunal
Bakery	Boulangerie	Factory	Usine
Bank	Banque	Fire station	Caserne de pompiers
Bookstore	Librairie	Florist	Fleuriste
Bus stop	Arrêt de bus	Gas station	Station-service
Butcher	Boucher	Grocery	Épicerie
Café	Café (lieu)	Gym	Salle de sport
Car park	Parking	Hospital	Hôpital
Church	Église	Hotel	Hôtel

Page 39 **Places & Buildings 2**

Library	Bibliothèque	School	École
Launderette	Laverie automatique	Skating rink	Patinoire
Mosque	Mosquée	Stadium	Stade
Museum	Musée	Station	Gare
Park	Parc	Supermarket	Supermarché
Pharmacy	Pharmacie	Synagogue	Synagogue
Playground	Terrain de jeu	Temple	Temple
Police station	Commissariat	Theater	Théâtre
Post office	Bureau de poste	Town hall	Mairie
Restaurant	Restaurant	University	Université

Page 40 **Parts of the house 1**

Attic	Grenier	Dining room	Salle à manger
Balcony	Balcon	Door	Porte
Basement	Sous-sol	Driveway	Allée
Bathroom	Salle de bains	Fence	Clôture
Bedroom	Chambre	Floor	Plancher
Ceiling	Plafond	Garage	Garage
Cellar	Cave	Garden	Jardin
Chimney	Cheminée de toit	Gate	Portail
Conservatory	Véranda	Greenhouse	Serre
Corridor	Couloir	Ground floor	Rez-de-chaussée

Page 41 **Parts of the house 2**

Guest room	Chambre d'amis	Porch	Porche
Gutter	Gouttière	Roof	Toit
Hall	Hall	Shed	Cabane
House	Maison	Shutter	Volet
Kitchen	Cuisine	Stairs	Escaliers
Letterbox	Boîte aux lettres	Swimming pool	Piscine
Living room	Séjour	Toilet	Toilettes
Lounge	Salon	Utility room	Buanderie
Path	Chemin	Wall	Mur
Patio	terrasse	Window	Fenêtre

Lexique

Page 42 **Living room**

Armchair	Fauteuil	Painting	Tableau
Blind	Store	Air conditioner	Climatiseur
Carpet	Moquette	Radiator	Radiateur
Coffee table	Table basse	Remote	Télécommande
Curtains	Rideaux	Rug	tapis
Cushion	Coussin	Shelves	Étagères
Fan	Ventilateur	Sofa	Canapé
Fireplace	Cheminée	Stool	Tabouret
Footrest	Repose-pied	Television	Télévision
Furniture	Mobilier	Vase	Vase

Page 43 **Bedroom**

Alarm clock	Réveil	Hanger	Cintre
Bed	Lit	Headboard	Tête de lit
Bed base	Sommier	Lamp	Lampe
Bedside lamp	Lampe de chevet	Mattress	Matelas
Bedside table	Table de chevet	Pillow	Oreiller
Blanket	Couverture	Pillowcase	Taie d'oreiller
Bunk beds	Lits superposés	Sheet	Drap
Chest of drawers	Commode	Single bed	Lit simple
Double bed	Lit double	Sofa bed	Canapé-lit
Duvet	Couette	Wardrobe	Armoire

Page 44 **Kitchen 1**

Apron	Tablier	Dishwasher	Lave-vaisselle
Blender	Mélangeur	Fork	Fourchette
Bowl	Bol	Freezer	Congélateur
Chopping board	Planche à découper	Fridge	Réfrigérateur
Coffee maker	Cafetière	Frying pan	Poêle
Colander	Passoire	Glass	Verre
Cooker	Cuisinière	Grater	Râpe
Cooker hood	Hotte	Hob	Plaque de cuisson
Cup	Tasse	Kettle	Bouilloire
Cupboard	Placard	Kitchen paper	Essuie-tout

Page 45 **Kitchen 2**

Knife	Couteau	Saucepan	Casserole
Ladle	Louche	Scale	Balance
Microwave	Micro-ondes	Sink	Évier
Napkin	Serviette de table	Spoon	Cuillère
Oven	Four	Tablespoon	Cuillère à soupe
Oven glove	Gant de four	Tea towel	Torchon
Plate	Assiette	Teapot	Théière
Pressure cooker	Cocotte minute	Teaspoon	Cuillère à café
Rollin pin	Rouleau à pâtisserie	Toaster	Grille-pain
Salad bowl	Saladier	Worktop	Plan de travail

Lexique

Page 46 **Bathroom**

Bath mat	Tapis de bain	Razor	Rasoir
Bathrobe	Peignoir	Shampoo	Shampooing
Bathtub	Baignoire	Shower	Douche
Brush	Brosse	Shower curtain	Rideau de douche
Comb	Peigne	Soap	Savon
Cotton bud	Coton-tige	Tap	Robinet (GB)
Faucet	Robinet (USA)	Toothbrush	Brosse à dents
Hair dryer	Sèche-cheveux	Toothpaste	Dentifrice
Make-up	Maquillage	Towel	Serviette
Mirror	Miroir	Washbasin	Lavabo

Page 47 **Utility room**

Bleach	Eau de javel	Ironing board	Planche à repasser
Boiler	Chaudière	laundry basket	Panier à linge
Broom	Balai	Mop	Serpillère
Bucket	Seau	Plunger	Ventouse
Circuit breaker	Disjoncteur	Recycling bin	Poubelle tri sélectif
Clotheshorse	Étendoir	Stepladder	Escabeau
Clothespin	Pince à linge	Toolbox	Caisse à outils
Detergent	Détergent	Tumble dryer	Sèche-linge
Dustpan	Pelle	Vacuum	Aspirateur
Iron	Fer à repasser	Washing machine	Machine à laver

Page 48 **On the road**

Bridge	Pont	Pedestrian	Piéton
Crosswalk	Passage piéton	Roundabout	Rond-point
Cycle path	Piste cyclable	Shoulder	Bande d'arrêt d'urgence
Exit	Sortie	Sign	Panneau
Fire hydrant	Bouche d'incendie	Street	Rue
Highway	Autoroute	Toll	Péage
Lamppost	Lampadaire	Traffic jam	Embouteillage
Manhole	Bouche d'égout	Traffic lights	Feu de circulation
One-way street	Sens unique	Tunnel	Tunnel
Pavement	Trottoir	Underpass	Passage souterrain

Page 49 **Means of transport**

Bike	Vélo	Rocket	Fusée
Boat	Bateau	Scooter	Trotinette
Bus	Bus	Ship	Navire
Car	Voiture	Skateboard	Skateboard
Caravan	Caravane	Submarine	Sous-marin
Helicopter	Hélicoptère	Subway	Métro (USA)
Lorry	Camion (GB)	Train	Train
Moped	Mobylette	Truck	Camion (USA)
Motorcycle	Moto	Underground	Métro(GB)
Plane	Avion	Van	Camionnette

Lexique

Page 50 **Car parts**

Battery	Batterie	Indicator	Clignotant
Bumper	Pare-chocs	License plate	Plaque d'immatriculation
Clutch	Embrayage	Rearview mirror	Rétroviseur
Dashboard	Tableau de bord	Seat	Siège
Engine	Moteur	Seat belt	Ceinture de sécurité
Exhaust pipe	Pot déchappement	Steering wheel	Volant
Gear lever	Levier de vitesse	Tire	Pneu
Glove compartment	Boîte à gants	Wheel	Roue
Handbrake	Frein à main	Windshield	Pare-brise
Horn	Klaxon	Wiper	Essuie-glace

Page 51 **Tools**

Adjustable wrench	Clé à molette	Pliers	Pince
Axe	Hache	Rake	Râteau
Cutter	Cutter	Saw	Scie
Drill	Perceuse	Screwdriver	Tournevis
Hammer	Marteau	Shears	Cisaille
Hose	Tuyau d'arrosage	Shovel	Pelle
Ladder	Échelle	Spirit level	Niveau à bulle
Lawn mower	Tondeuse	Tape measure	Mètre à ruban
Mallet	Maillet	Torch	Torche
Pickaxe	Pioche	Wheelbarrow	Brouette

Solutions

Days & Months

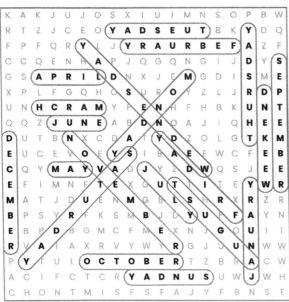

Weather

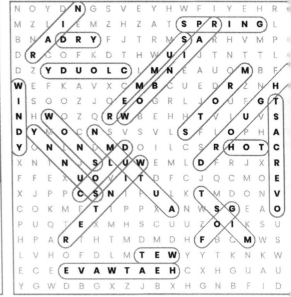

Numbers

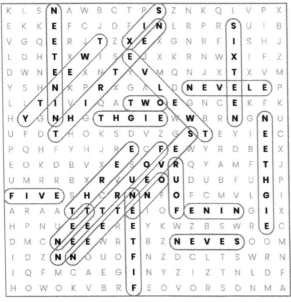

Colors

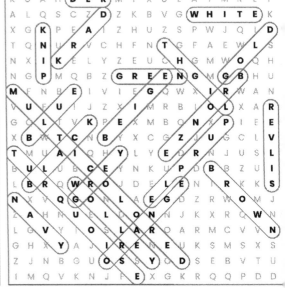

Solutions

Common Verbs

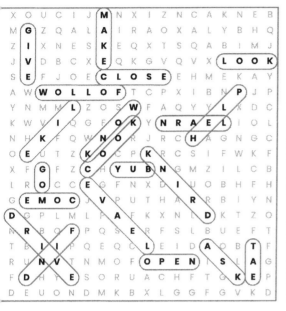

Common Verbs

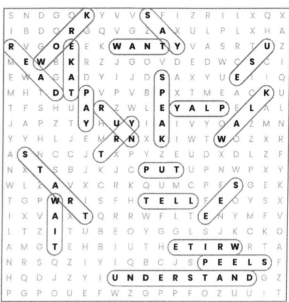

Preposition of place

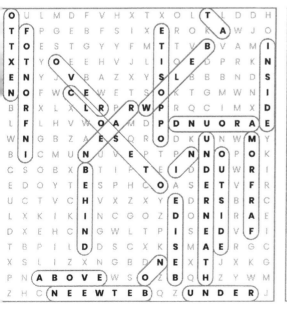

Family

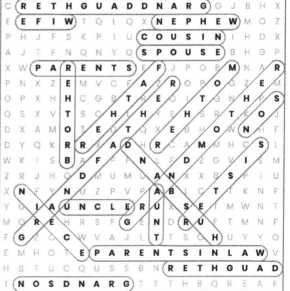

Solutions

The head

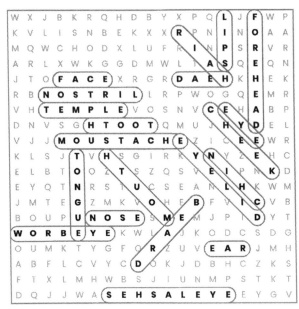

The body

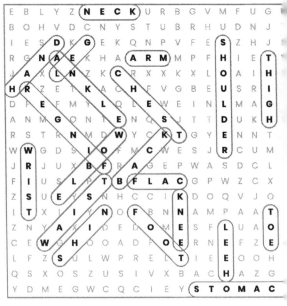

Physical Appearance

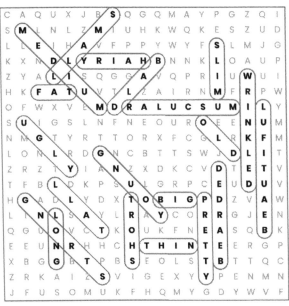

Characters

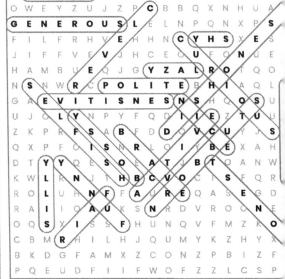

Solutions

Feelings 1

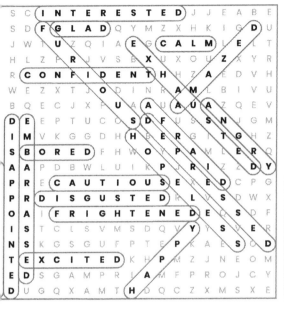

Feelings 2

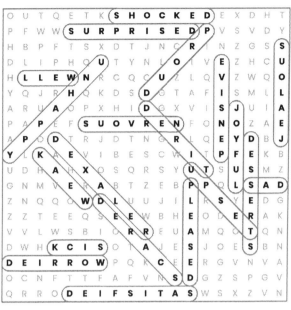

Restaurant

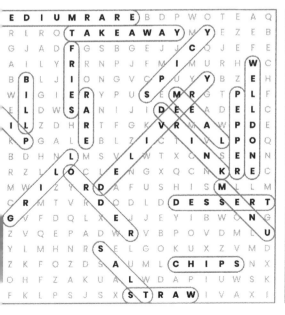

Food

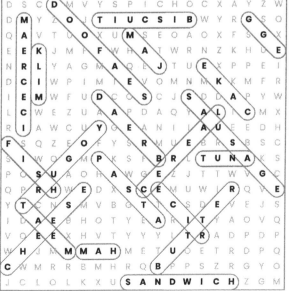

Solutions

Fruits 1

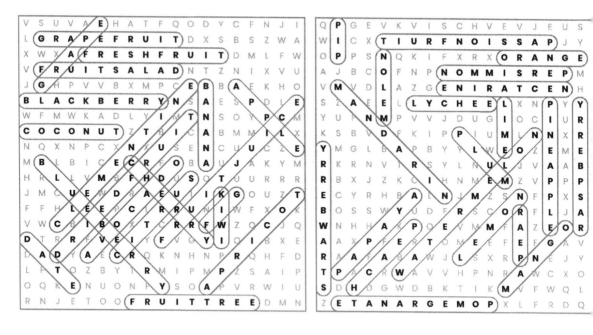

Fruits 2

Vegetables 1

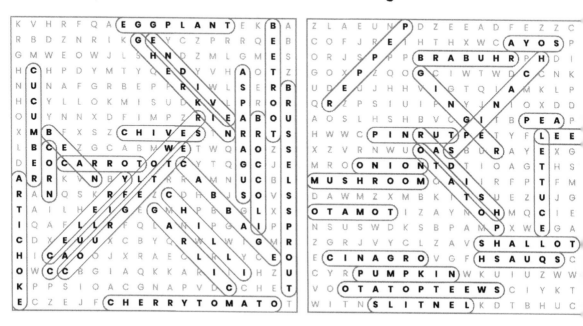

Vegetables 2

Solutions

Pets & Farm animals

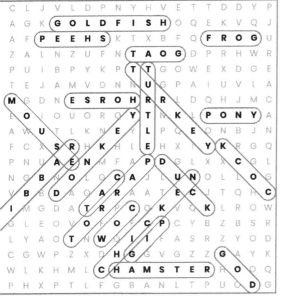

Wild animals

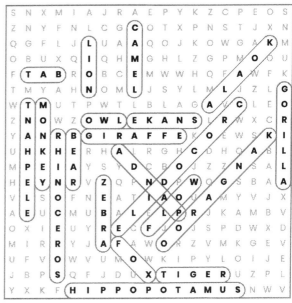

Insects

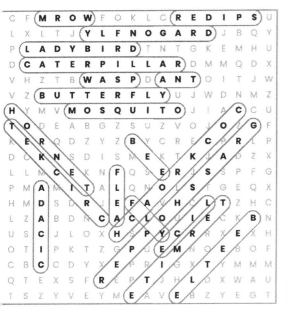

Hobbies

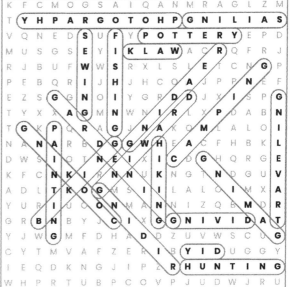

Solutions

Jobs 1

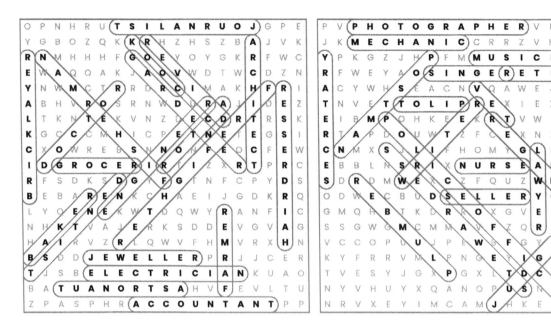

Jobs 2

The classroom 1

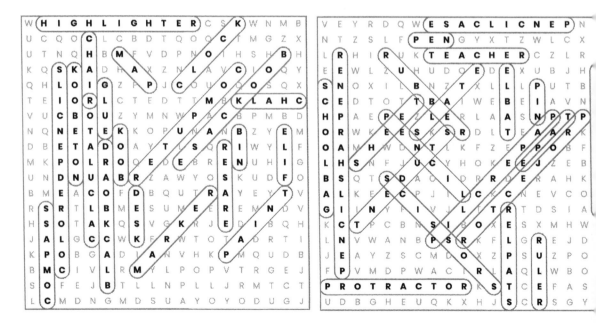

The classroom 2

Solutions

Exam

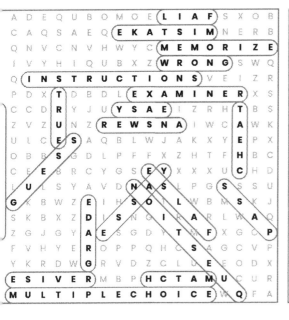

Shopping

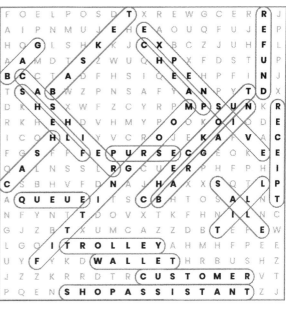

Clothes 1

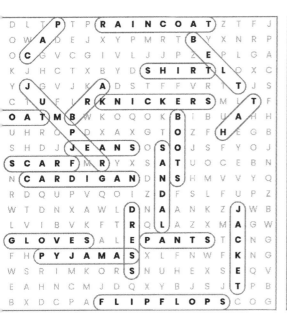

Clothes 2

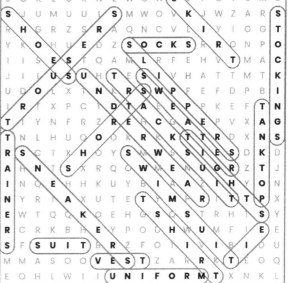

Solutions

Nature

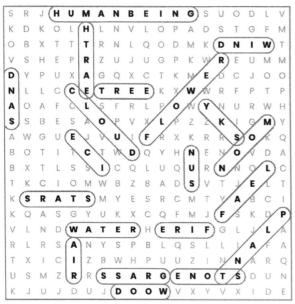

Landscape

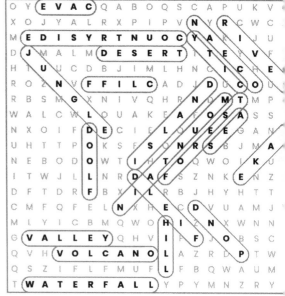

Travel 1

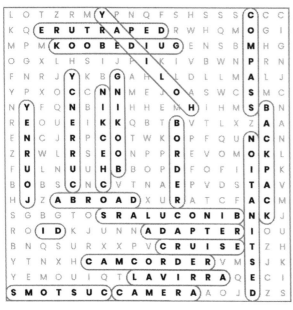

Travel 2

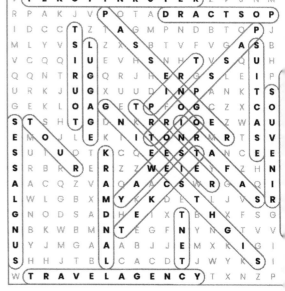

Solutions

Places & Buildings 1

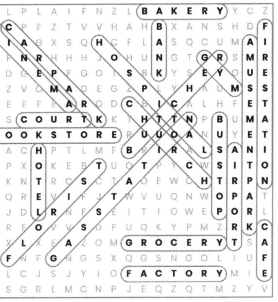

Places & Buildings 2

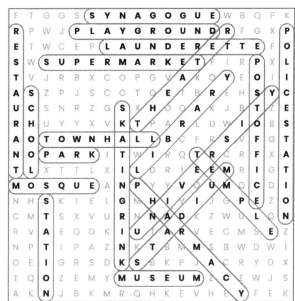

Parts of the house 1

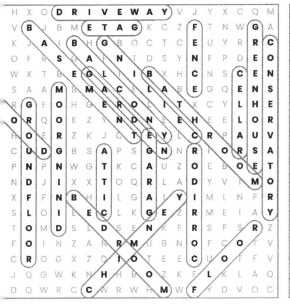

Parts of the house 2

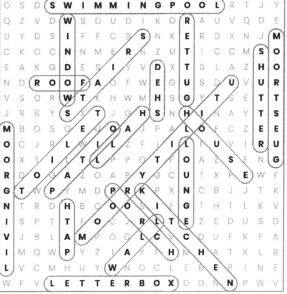

Solutions

Living room

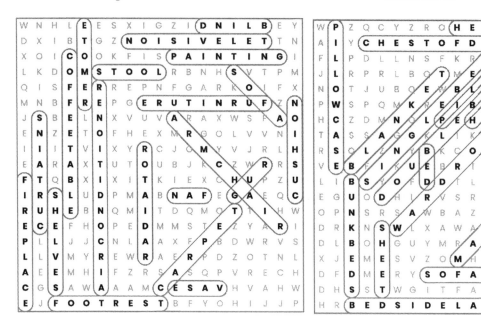

Bedroom

Kitchen 1

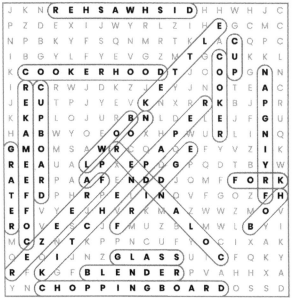

Kitchen 2

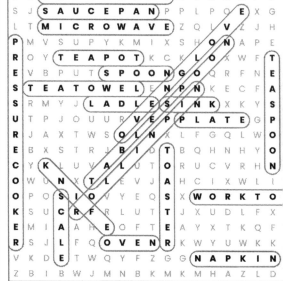

Solutions

Bathroom

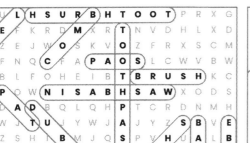

Utility room

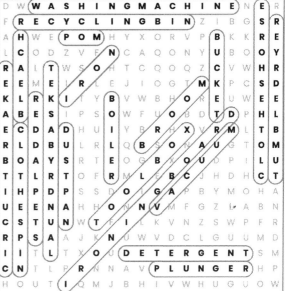

On the road

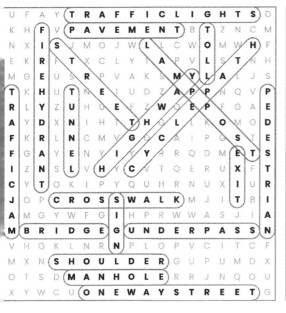

Means of transport

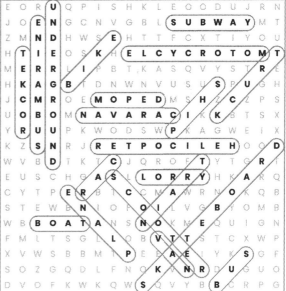

Solutions

Car parts

Tools

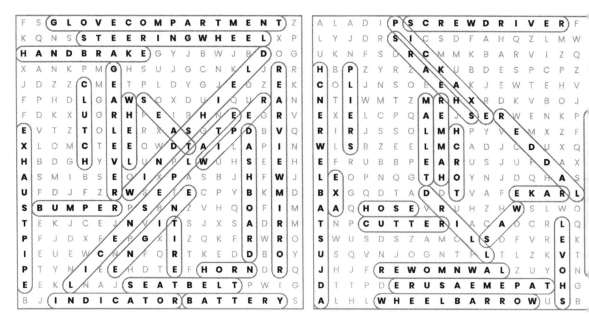

Notes

Notes

Notes

Printed in France by Amazon
Brétigny-sur-Orge, FR

19456343R00047